God's People and the Seduction of Empire

Hearing God's call in the modern age

— GRAHAM TURNER —

Sacristy Press
PO Box 612, Durham, DH1 9HT

www.sacristy.co.uk

First published in 2016 by Sacristy Press, Durham

Copyright © Graham Turner 2016
The moral rights of the author have been asserted

Sacristy Limited, registered in England & Wales, number 7565667

British Library Cataloguing-in-Publication Data
A catalogue record for the book is available from the British Library

ISBN 978-1-910519-00-4

Foreword

Anything that is big—a noble idea, a financial organization, a welfare system, a powerful country, a global religion—has the potential to do great good but also great harm. Large bureaucracies enable our homes, cars and lives to be insured, thus preventing minor accidents from becoming major financial catastrophes. They enable us to eat in complete confidence food prepared by total strangers, to enjoy clean water and abundant energy, to fly safely in metal tubes thousands of feet above the ground, to provide quality health care to all, to manage pension systems providing reliable income support to the elderly, and to borrow money at reasonable interest rates for everything from higher education to a new house. The everyday conveniences of modern life would not be possible without them.

Left to its own devices, however, big-ness too frequently becomes "empire", an instrument of domination, exclusion and suppression. As Graham Turner argues in this compelling book, God's vision since the beginning of time and still today is radically different: a "kingdom" characterized by diversity, inclusion, and liberation. The perennial challenge is how to actively resist the enduring temptations of empire while arraying against it a series of countervailing forces enabling the virtues of scale to offset its many vices. On a good day, law and democracy play these roles in secular life: an effective legal system ensures the same rules apply to princes and paupers alike; regular elections ensure those wielding political power answer to the collective voice of the citizenry, that majorities don't suppress minorities (and vice versa). On a bad day, however, law becomes itself an instrument of empire, enabling the powerful to consolidate their interests and silence their critics, while elections get highjacked, held merely to confer an air of legitimacy on those openly using the public purse to indulge and consolidate their private privilege.

At its best, the Judeo-Christian tradition has sought to tame the imperatives of empire via two complementary strategies: urging people of faith to live a life authentically consistent with "kingdom" values of prudence, forgiveness and generosity (no matter how foolish or futile this may seem), while also organizing politically to promote justice with and for the poor. The former strategy operates at the personal level, ensuring that stated belief and lived behaviour are minimally consistent; the latter is a collective task, an overt act of solidarity with those who regularly find themselves on the losing side of struggles with powerful people, companies, governments and sometimes even their own families and communities. The God of both the Hebrew and Christian scriptures seeks justice and mercy, not elaborate ceremonies, and assesses any given society by the quality of life enjoyed by its most marginal members. But realising those ends is perpetually aspirational precisely because the logic of empire routinely and relentlessly intervenes.

At this key juncture in the life of the church—the end of "Christendom" and the emergence of an increasingly influential "postmodern" culture—Turner provides an honest, accurate and inspiring accounting of where the Church has come from, where it's at, and where it needs to go if it is to thwart empire's twenty-first-century manifestations. It is perhaps no accident that today's empires have it within them to actually end hunger and premature death for all, while also having the capacity to fry the planet or blow it up hundreds of times over. Which will it be? The challenge, as always, is to love what God loves, to learn to see and hear what those on the margins are teaching us, and to remain unafraid of "death", knowing that it is the necessary prelude to bountiful resurrection.

Michael Woolcock
Kuala Lumpur, April 2016

Michael Woolcock is Lead Social Development Specialist with the World Bank's Development Research Group, and a Lecturer in Public Policy at Harvard University's Kennedy School of Government.

Preface

The Bible is a difficult book. Nobody told me this, because it was God's book. I grew up with all the exciting stories of the Old and New Testaments, but no one drew my attention to the hard and incomprehensible bits. We skirted round these. As a young adult, I thought I needed to learn from those who already knew about the Bible—Bible teachers, theologians and those who wrote books about the Bible. Then one day, when I had properly absorbed all they knew, I would understand how it all fitted together. I would be "in the know" as they were "in the know". When I was thirty-five, and nearly ten years into full-time ministry, I realised, maybe rather late in the day, this was never going to happen. I started to meet other people who said, "The Bible is a very hard book to get your head round." Some of these were church members, some were colleagues and some were theologians. Mistakenly, I had grown up in the church with the impression there was a great body of wisdom and truth which my elders would simply pass down to me, from on high. If I worked hard at receiving this, then the fog would clear.

Then I heard about people who dealt with the Bible quite differently. They were Christians in South America who were no longer content to unquestioningly accept from their elders what the message of the Bible was. An interpretation of the Bible from a quite different European context did not fit their experience of life in Peru, Brazil, El Salvador or Uruguay. These Christians insisted that where we live and how we live have an important part to play in how we understand the Bible. They said a culture, a community's story and its situation in life, all have a part to play in trying to work out what the message was for us, here today. Bible scholars and theologians are not irrelevant, but they are only part of the picture.

When I look back, my story has always affected my choices in life, including how I viewed the Bible. I warmed to some of its characters more than others and related to some of its ideas more than others, because they made some sort of link to my experiences. One great shadow in my life was my schooling. My primary school was a fairly peaceful and sweet existence that did not prepare me in any way for the hell-hole that was to be my secondary school. My first day, in what was to become the biggest all-boys school in Britain of the late 1960s, was a terrifying shock to me. I was immersed into a world of violence, fear, bullying and abuse, by both older boys and some staff members. The only way for me to survive was to find my place in the pecking order of the playground, making sure those above me did not beat me up too often and that I oppressed those below me so they did not usurp my position.

On Sundays I went to church, sometimes three times. I was told about the love of Jesus. I was very strongly encouraged to be a witness about my faith during the week. I prayed, read my Bible (now and again), sung the hymns and songs, and gave my all to being a church Christian. On Monday morning I returned to the nightmare which was school. I was aware of one boy getting badly beaten up for being a vicar's son. Any differences or weaknesses were homed in on by the bigger and more powerful boys. Even listening to the music of T. Rex was enough to get a good thrashing; Led Zeppelin and Hawkwind were the right bands to follow. I worked out that witnessing to Jesus was not a clever thing to do if I wanted to keep my few friends and my teeth. I said almost nothing to those in school about Jesus and I said little to anyone outside the school about the violence I encountered during the week. As I took part in the violence as much as anyone else, I could not easily blow the whistle on what went on.

At the weekend, I was to be found back in church singing to Jesus, in whom I really believed. When I was thirteen, something happened that shook me to the core. My closest friend at the Sunday afternoon boys' Bible class suddenly died as a result of a congenital heart condition. None of us knew of his illness. Through this crisis of loss I became even more convinced about the Jesus of the Bible; I wanted to follow him, but each Monday I returned to a different reality. The situation at the school was so serious that some years after I left one boy stabbed and killed another pupil from his year group.

Looking back, I realise the discontinuity between my weekday life and my weekend life has had a major impact on my life and my faith. It is not that I am still wounded and disabled by it, but more the fact that I (almost subconsciously) always want to reduce the gap between such different worlds. I do not want to harmonise everything and remove all tension and difference, but I want to eliminate all unnecessary barriers that stop people being open to consider all Jesus stands for. The life of my church with its worship was good in some ways as it helped to nurture my faith. But it did not have anything to say, offer or demonstrate to my friends (and enemies) while I was at school. The issue here is not relevance, but authenticity. Our mission is not to sweeten the pill so it is easier for others to consider what Jesus says. Most people immediately see through this. Our mission is to be authentically God's people; people with integrity. I find it a little easier to be persecuted and vilified for believing in Jesus' life, death and resurrection if these make a true connection to the world of people I meet each day. What I find hard to bear is being mocked and maligned for some crazy things that have been (and are still) said, sung or done in the name of the church or God.

Most of my ordained ministry has been in less privileged communities. I spent five years living in the middle of a council estate in Leeds. This was then followed by twenty years in a predominantly Muslim community in Birmingham which scored highly on all indicators of social and economic deprivation. In these challenging situations a small band of us worked extremely hard to grow and develop the church. We poured our hearts into it as if there was nothing else to live for. We followed all the trends and current ideas about mission that were being promoted by the diocese, para-church movements and the larger, more influential churches. We were active and busy implementing all these ideas. At the end of the day, I have to be honest all this effort produced little fruit. Because of this, a number of us suffered burn-out and some became seriously ill. What worked for bigger churches did not work for us. What was successful for the latest Christian guru travelling around church networks was not successful for us. It felt as if the agenda of some parts of the broader church was being imposed upon us, if not directly then certainly by implication.

Our experience was that most of the tactics used in more middle-class parishes simply did not work in these poorer communities.

I had unquestioningly believed that "out there" somewhere was the answer to mission and ministry, whatever the context I found myself in. All I had to do was to find who had it, learn it from them and then implement it. This was when I heard about the alternative approach developed by Christians in South America. Up to this point, I had been trapped in a way of thinking which relied on finding "the" magical answer to ministry which would make it all work. If I could just download this way of thinking into my head, then my ministry would be transformed. But my painful experience of finding out this approach to ministry was not working forced me to reassess this view. I began to question whether those who I thought had the answers really had them. Had I been unfair in my expectations of them? I had fallen into the trap of assuming that if I got the theory right, then the implementation would follow relatively simply.

In time I realised most of the answers I looked for were to be found more locally, among unexpected people. My experience of living and working in less affluent communities was affecting me. If I allowed it, it could give me a completely new set of questions to ask of the Bible and the world. Over the years I have had conversations with a wide range of people: locals and those from overseas; theologians and "ordinary" Christians; people from other denominations and traditions; and even people from other faiths. I have read their books and listened to them speak. What I found out was that authentic faith and belief are very much shaped by where we live and whom we relate to. This is especially true when working in less privileged communities.

This book sums up how I now understand the story of the Bible in the light of this journey. To adopt the parlance, it is the hermeneutical lens through which I make sense of the text. It is an understanding I would never have considered or thought about thirty years ago. It is not only about personal faith; it is also about how we live together in societies which promote healthy communities and justice for everybody. I have found the Bible does not ask us to grow our churches, but to live as examples in the world of how things should be—in the kingdom of God. It asks us to identify what the gods of our age are and whether we have signed our loyalty over to them or not. The story of the Bible asks us to be, at times, a subversive people; not being prepared to do things the way the establishment wants them done. It implores us to take seriously the Ten Commandments with their call for worship of God, Sabbath rest and neighbourliness. I have discovered the Bible calls us out of the ways of empire (which are as dominant today as they have ever been) to live God's alternative way.

The Bible now seems more relevant to the boys I went to school with all those years ago. I have asked some questions about power and domination they might have asked had they been given the opportunity. The Bible is even more fascinating now than when I started. I have to say, though, it remains a difficult book.

I spent ten years serving as Team Rector in the relatively affluent market town of Macclesfield. This context also enabled me to ask questions about my time in Birmingham and gave me the distance to reflect a little more objectively on all that happened there. I am now a prison chaplain. This quite different setting is giving me a fresh opportunity to critique my ministry and provide me with new insights and understandings about the Bible. What I remain convinced about is this: the lessons that are being learnt in the poorer contexts for ministry need to be taught in the more wealthy churches and communities. If there is wisdom to be passed on we should not first look to the top and the centre, but to the margins and the bottom.

Acknowledgements

Some years ago I ran a Lent course on the theme of empires and the Bible. My good friend Cliff Mills said to me, "You must write this stuff up." But I thought I was not a writer. Then my colleague, Dave Mock, said, "Give me your notes and I'll have a go at doing a bit of it." As soon as I saw what he came up with, I saw how I could do it. So thanks to both Cliff and Dave for giving me the push I needed to get started.

Along the way there have been so many people, mainly from Macclesfield, who encouraged me, read chapters and made suggestions, spell-checked proofs and promised to buy the book when it eventually came out. Thanks to you all, you know who you are.

Special thanks go to Sue Reid who has done an enormous job. As well as being one of the band who have checked scripts, she has tenaciously hunted down the permissions required for the works I have quoted.

Richard Hilton and Thomas Ball of Sacristy Press have always been gracious, provided a professional service and taken the risk with me as a new author—many thanks.

My biggest thanks go to my family: to Rosie, who repeatedly supports me in my madcap ideas and has always believed in this book, and also to Adrian, Becca and Jon who still seem to believe that the "old man" might still have something interesting to say.

Contents

CHAPTER 1

Do not Follow the Way of Empire

In this book I will explain to you the interpretive lens through which I view the Bible. This lens is heavily coloured by the language of empires and kingdoms, emperors, pharaohs and kings. At first this might sound a lot like Dungeons & Dragons: mysterious other worlds to which we do not belong. But we do belong to a world of competing powers and global empires. The Bible uses the language of empires and kingdoms to represent these. As I talk about empires continually throughout this book, you may feel I overdo it. However, Jesus himself repeatedly used an equivalent term to empire: "kingdom". I therefore feel I am in good company.

My argument is this: the empires of the world nearly always end up opposed, in spirit and action, to the kingdom of God that is so central to Jesus' message. Occasionally there have been some exceptions, throughout the centuries, when empires and their emperors have been indifferent or even benevolent. These have been few and far between, however. Therefore, when I use the term "empire", it is usually in a negative and pejorative sense.

In this book, "empire" refers to power systems and ways of organising that tend to dominate and exploit. As Lord Acton's saying goes, "Power tends to corrupt, and absolute power corrupts absolutely". Thus, empires tend to seize control, dominate and manipulate. Nations, communities, organisations and corporations which enjoy power and wealth seem to want even more of the same, often at the expense of weaker and more vulnerable economies and poorer communities.

Empires are not just something God's people grappled with in the past. We also deal daily with empires which exploit those who are weaker. They threaten the environment, amass wealth for a few and contradict, or even simply ignore, all that we as people of faith hold dear. They pay no faithful attention to God, as, in the end, they create their own gods. We see them in retail empires (e.g., large supermarket chains; giant on-line retailers), economic empires (e.g., banks; financial markets) and cultural empires (e.g., languages; film and digital media). While not everything empires do is bad, they do have an in-built tendency to dominate, control and exploit. The Bible points out that this is simply not God's way of doing things.

The history of humankind has sadly been a catalogue of who killed whom and which empire succeeded the previous one. Violence, force and bullying have fuelled the life of the empires. The violence may not always have been physical; it has often been economic or cultural. It has always been destructive, however, and those with less power are those who have ultimately lost out.

I have come to the conclusion that God's invitation, spelled out throughout the Bible, is to live in a completely different way—not just as individuals, but as nations, communities, families, economies, cultures and churches. Jesus calls this other way "the kingdom of God" (or the kingdom of heaven in Matthew's Gospel). His mission was not to make people Christians; neither was St Paul's, nor the early church's. Jesus came to establish a different way of living and ordering life which was in stark contrast to the established ways of the world, with their imperial ways of living. This different way has its roots far back in history in a fresh and radical application of the Ten Commandments, and in Abraham. Therefore, let us start with Abraham before his name was changed by God.

Abram

The story of Israel begins with Abram. In the book of Genesis, other stories are written before the accounts of Abram's life—but these are a different sort of literature, written for a different purpose. I will return to a few of these stories a little later.

Abram was called to set out on an adventure, leave the city of Ur and travel to a new land:

> Now the Lord said to Abram, "Go from your country and your kindred and your father's house to the land that I will show you. I will make of you a great nation, and I will bless you, and make your name great, so that you will be a blessing. I will bless those who bless you, and the one who curses you I will curse; and in you all the families of the earth shall be blessed." (Gen. 12:1–3)

The city he left was as significant as the new country he travelled to. Ur was a city in the ancient empire of Babylon. Babylon saw itself as being a great and mighty power. It created enormous wealth for a number of its citizens while at the same time exploiting and enslaving thousands upon thousands for its benefit.

Abram was called away from this pattern of living with its injustices and worship of gods who endorsed dominative and fear-based practices. Abram was led out of this so-called civilisation to the relatively backward hill country of Canaan in what is now Palestine/Israel. The God who called Abram was different to the gods of his family's empire—this God was called "Yahweh".

In calling Abram, this God made a counter-promise to that made by Babylon. He said he would make Abram a great nation *outside* of empire. While Babylon was regarded as the greatest nation on earth, God said to Abram he would make him a great nation, but not by using the tactics and schemes of empire. Abram therefore left all Babylon promised and trusted the word and provision of God. He took with him his wife, Sarah, his nephew, Lot, and all the members of his household. With this small community, Abram was to learn to live in a "non-imperial" way of life.

They had not been in Canaan very long when they encountered their first crisis—hunger. Genesis tells us there was a famine in the land (Gen. 12:10), and soon Abram found it hard to trust God's promise, "I will make of you a great nation, and I will bless you" (Gen. 12:2). His fears got the better of him, and now being a nomad, he did what nomads do—he moved on, eventually to Egypt, the other great empire in the region. Abram chose to return to the promise of empire over and against the promise of God.

He soon discovered that in choosing empire, with all its enticements, his problems started to multiply. Now, adrift from God, he was left to his own devices, or so it felt. He worried about his own safety and what might happen to his attractive wife, Sarah. In order to save his own life, Abram passed Sarah off as his sister. If he had admitted she was his wife, then the Egyptians may well have killed him and taken her. Instead, he allowed her to be taken into Pharaoh's (Emperor's) household as one of his wives, where she had no rights or status and so no protection. As a result of Abram's scheming, Sarah was sexually compromised in order to save his skin.

Not before too long, Pharaoh and his court were afflicted with a sickness. Pharaoh was now worried. He blamed Abram. "What have you done to us? Why didn't you tell me she was your wife?" (Gen. 12:18) As a result, Abram, together with his people, was thrown out of Egypt.

Abram was called out of one empire, Babylon, only to be seduced by the next one he came across, Egypt. He was obedient in obeying the initial call, but found learning to trust God's alternative way was not so easy.

Famine and Egypt again

Abram's name was changed to Abraham and his son, Isaac, was born. God renewed his promise:

> I will indeed bless you, and I will make your offspring as
> numerous as the stars of heaven and as the sand that is on
> the seashore. And your offspring shall possess the gate of
> their enemies, and by your offspring shall all the nations
> of the earth gain blessing for themselves, because you have
> obeyed my voice. (Gen. 22:17–18)

In Genesis 26 we read the adult Isaac was told not to go down to Egypt. To his credit, when hunger came his way, he stayed away. He remained in Canaan, obeying God, despite the uncertainties of the food supply. However, this seemed to be a brief respite before empire called seductively again to the generations that followed, those from whom God wanted to make a nation.

We now fast-forward through the story of Jacob, one of Isaac's sons, to Joseph, Jacob's favourite son. Joseph, like Abraham, was a mixture of contradictions, able to trust and follow God, while also, at times, compromising himself in the business of empire. Being a favourite son, he was also, of course, a despised brother. His siblings got the better of him. They captured him and sold him on as a slave to traders who were on their way to Egypt. It is a fascinating story how he rose from being an abused slave in an army officer's house to become an imperial ruler, "Prime Minister" in Egypt. He was second-in-command to Pharaoh. It is here we see Joseph also adopt the ways of empire.

It happened that his family back in Canaan and the ordinary people of Egypt had no food: another famine had hit the region. Interestingly, however, Pharaoh had food. We might therefore ask how it was Pharaoh had food when the rest of the population did not. We might answer that it was because Joseph was a shrewd and efficient imperial administrator, or else that it is the nature of empires to hoard resources for themselves; resources which should really be shared. I am of the opinion that Pharaoh's greed probably caused the regional famine in the first place.

This is how the story unfolded back then (Gen. 47:1–26). Hungry people came from Canaan and the districts of Egypt to Joseph to buy food. Eventually they had spent all their money purchasing supplies. They then came to Joseph and said, "We need more food, but we have no money." Joseph said there was still food to be bought, but only if they gave Pharaoh their livestock as payment. As they were hungry, they agreed. When all their money was spent and all their livestock had been taken, the people cried out, "There is nothing left but our bodies and our land." They were still hungry. Joseph therefore took all their land as payment for yet more food. Joseph and Pharaoh had taken from them their only means of making a living. At first it looks as if Joseph was serving the people and their best interests, but in reality he was gradually enslaving them. This is one of the traits of empire.

In the end, the people had nothing left with which to buy food. They said, "You have saved our lives; may it please my lord, we will be slaves to Pharaoh" (Gen. 47:25). The people came looking for food but ended up as slaves. They innocently thought it would be good and generous of Pharaoh if he could make them his slaves. Empires enslave us without us even realising it, or when we think (mistakenly) our best interests are being served. (It is worth noting that the priests of Egypt were not enslaved. Pharaoh needed the backing of the gods in order to assert what he did was divinely endorsed.)

Slaves in Egypt

In the wake of Joseph's story, there was no freedom for the descendants of Abraham. At the beginning of the book of Exodus we learn there was a new Pharaoh in Egypt who further enslaved the Israelites as labourers and brick makers for the empire's massive building projects. God's people had become too numerous and a threat to the empire. Pharaoh's response was not to integrate the Israelites and their cultural life into Egypt, thus making it a more diverse and arguably stronger nation; he saw them as a threat, so exploited them as an economic resource.

When Moses arrived as the bearer of God's voice, slavery was well established. Following his own turbulent journey into adulthood, Moses petitioned Pharaoh to allow the people go into the wilderness for three days to celebrate a festival (Exod. 5). This was a non-violent action against the empire. They asked just for a few days off to act out their cultural and religious rituals beyond the influence of Pharaoh and his imperial cult.[1] Through this action, the Israelites sought to honour another God, not the gods of Egypt.

Pharaoh recognised rebellion when he saw it. This was a defiant act of resistance. It was a request for rest from work—Sabbath rest. If Pharaoh allowed this it would have set a terrible precedent and he would have lost control over the enslaved masses. Pharaoh's response was instead to increase the terms of slavery. The people were forced to make bricks while also gathering their own straw. As a result they had to build the magnificent structures of Egypt more quickly and contributed to the cost out of their own poverty.

Wherever you get empires you get enslaved people "making bricks" (or the equivalent) for imperial projects. When I visit great palaces, temples and buildings during day trips out, or while on holiday, I often get a very uneasy feeling. Most of them have been built on the backs of the poor, either through cheap labour, heavy taxation or enforced slavery. They may be magnificent, but someone, somewhere, has paid a high price for their construction.

Pharaoh's economy was not about prosperity for everyone. His plan, like those of most emperors, was to accumulate ever-increasing wealth for a small powerful elite. Other smaller stakeholders might benefit from this, but only incidentally and rarely deliberately.

Sinai (Exodus 19–24)

After a period of painful protest and confrontation, the people of God were freed from Egypt. More significantly, they were freed from slavery and oppression, a point they would be continually reminded of throughout their history. Passover became the great festival which celebrated this rescue from empire. It was the festival at which Jesus was crucified. Paul referred to Jesus as the Passover Lamb. Today, Jews still celebrate the Passover festival. The exodus, when this vulnerable community made its escape from a sophisticated empire into a desert wilderness, is one of the most important historical events of the Old Testament.

So, as powerless people, the Children of Israel travelled and camped in harsh landscapes until they came to Mount Sinai. This is where Moses received a revelation from God. This brought the hope that the Israelites might become a different sort of community, a community whose patterns of life would be in stark contrast to the ways of Egypt and the other nations. Here, once again, was the call to become a great nation, just as had been made so many generations before to Abraham. This time there was to be a "foundational document" to set the course for God's people to live a different way. This document was called the Ten Commandments.

The Ten Commandments

Then God spoke all these words:

I am the Lord your God, who brought you out of the land of Egypt, out of the house of slavery; you shall have no other gods before me.

You shall not make for yourself an idol, whether in the form of anything that is in heaven above, or that is on the earth beneath, or that is in the water under the earth. You shall not bow down to them or worship them; for I the Lord your God am a jealous God, punishing children for the iniquity of parents, to the third and the fourth generation of those who reject me, but showing steadfast love to the thousandth generation of those who love me and keep my commandments.

You shall not make wrongful use of the name of the Lord your God, for the Lord will not acquit anyone who misuses his name.

Remember the sabbath day, and keep it holy. For six days you shall labour and do all your work. But the seventh day is a sabbath to the Lord your God; you shall not do any work—you, your son or your daughter, your male or female slave, your livestock, or the alien resident in your towns. For in six days the Lord made heaven and earth, the sea, and all that is in them, but rested the seventh day; therefore the Lord blessed the sabbath day and consecrated it.

Honour your father and your mother, so that your days may be long in the land that the Lord your God is giving you.

You shall not murder.

You shall not commit adultery.

You shall not steal.

You shall not bear false witness against your neighbour.

You shall not covet your neighbour's house; you shall not covet your neighbour's wife, or male or female slave, or ox, or donkey, or anything that belongs to your neighbour. (Exod. 20:1–17)

The Ten Commandments stand high above all the other laws and commands of the Old Testament. We know this because of the manner in which they were given. Before and after Moses received them, there was great drama and razzmatazz. This was a manifestation of God, sometimes called a *theophany*. There was thunder and lightening, quickly followed by dark clouds and the blast of a trumpet. The mountain was wrapped in smoke, "because the Lord had descended upon it with fire". The ground shook. It was as if God was saying, "This is really important; take note!"

At the very top of Mount Sinai, Moses met God and the Ten Commandments were given and received. This was the high point of God showing himself to his people in the Old Testament. From this point on, it was expected the Children of Israel would be a people who lived a different way.

The commandments set out how radically different God's approach to community living is from the seduction and oppression of empire. Such was the hope and expectation of what God would give the Israelites that they even said "yes" before they knew what would be asked of them (Exod. 19:8). They figured it must be better than the commandments of Pharaoh, which were: work harder, produce more, and serve the state. What was this new way?

It is probably true to say many of us have something of a love/hate relationship with the Ten Commandments. For those who are inclined to law keeping and structure, they have been clear markers along the way about what is right and what is wrong. For those whose lives are less aligned to structure and form, and who have a passion for freedom, they have seemed rather legalistic, restrictive and negative. Unfortunately, the first group of people have used the Ten Commandments as a measure of individual righteousness and personal morality, turning them into religious bigots. They have condemned those who have broken the laws and used them as a way of excluding others. The second group of people have tended to ignore them, or at least have been selective in how they have used them.

The Ten Commandments were given as foundational principles for the community so they could live a way of life which was a life-giving alternative to the death of empire. Today we have lost something of their radical edge. They are often reduced to a personal moral code against which we can measure our piety. They are not embraced as a profound alternative to the values and principles of today's economic and consumerist empires. We have reduced them to rules for individuals to obey. If there has to be a priority, I believe these commandments should be addressed first to the community before the individual. When society as a whole believes it has a right to kill people, it is no great surprise its citizens think they can do the same to their enemies. If the community clearly compromises its values by aligning itself with the empires and so is unfaithful to God, then it is no great surprise marriage partners may feel, from time to time, that unfaithfulness is not such a serious matter. How we act together influences how we act as individuals.

We need to reinstate the Ten Commandments as our foundational document in building different sorts of communities; communities which reject the ways of empire. We also need to recover their importance if we are to understand (as we will see later) how central they were to Jesus' teaching and his community, whom he calls to stand against the dominating powers of the empire and their seduction.

The first step in reclaiming the true authority of the Ten Commandments is to reinstate what is missing from them in the old Anglican prayer book and on the plaques which hang on church walls across Britain. The text actually says, "I am the Lord your God, *who brought you out of the land of Egypt, out of the house of slavery;* you shall have no other gods before me" (Exod. 20:2). The Book of Common Prayer and the hangings in our churches misleadingly omit the words I have emphasised in italics. One has to wonder why this happened. (It is good to see the Church of England has reinstated this phrase in its current services in Common Worship, however.)

What do the Ten Commandments do?

First, they look back: "I am the Lord your God, who brought you out of the land of Egypt, out of the house of slavery." God pointed out where they have come from and what they have been rescued from. They have been rescued from making bricks in Egypt; they have been rescued from miserable and demeaning slavery. Here at Mount Sinai, the Children of Israel are given the chance of another way.

Second, they are about relating to God. It is clear in the first commandment: the people should not have any other gods (Exod. 20:3)[2]. The second commandment states they should not give in to the temptation of idolatry by making their God appear like the things around them, as the Egyptians did. God cannot be captured in images constructed by humans. The presence of an image to represent God implies God is not present. I heard someone put it this way: "If my wife is away travelling I look at a picture of her, but if she is present I don't need the picture." In the full presence of God, Israel did not need images or concepts, as God was fully present to them. St Augustine said, "God is more in me than I am myself."

In the next commandment, the Children of Israel were commanded not to use the name of God in vain. There are two issues here. It is hard to trust ourselves to use the name of God completely seriously, without being, in any way, lighthearted, trite or familiar. However, in using the name of God at one level or another, the Israelites felt they would be taking it in vain. So it was never spoken. The other issue relates to our tendency to exploit a name. There is power in using a name. It is all too easy for us to co-opt God (by using God's name) to our self-serving projects or to support our self-image, our egos. God is not to be used for our own advantage in the market where reputations are traded. So Israel did not use the name "Yahweh". Instead there was silence, or just the sound of a breath. This was in contrast to Egypt, where all the gods were named and their names frequently spoken.

Third, the commandments are about neighbourliness. They are about how relationships should be ordered in the community so trust, mutuality and well-being benefit everyone—something they did not experience in Pharaoh's Egypt. Parents are to be honoured, not exploited. There is an obligation on the community to care for them as they become elderly. Neighbours should not be exploited for personal gain; other people should not be used as commodities. Their lives, spouses and property are not to be taken from them. What is said in court must not be twisted for personal gain or profit. The final commandment sums up all of these injunctions and points to the one of the great evils of Egypt that multiplied suffering—covetousness. Do not desire to have what others have, and do not want to be how others are. Jesus summarised the last five commandments in the seven words, "You shall love your neighbour as yourself" (Mark 12:31).

The empire always seemed to want more from its people in the form of ever-increasing productivity, and more from its territories with their natural and agricultural resources. It was always on the take. This approach to life does not build community but destroys it for most people.

You may have noticed there is one commandment I have not yet mentioned which, arguably, is the key to holding all the others together. It is the command to keep the Sabbath day; the fourth commandment. This was not new to Israel; it was supposed to have already been kept as Exodus 16:22–26 tells us. (It was even observed by the Egyptians during the more benign periods of their empire.) This primary commandment to keep the Sabbath stands in total opposition to the experience of the Children of Israel under empire. There they had no Sabbath and no enjoyment of rest. We will see later that the Sabbath principle was established at creation when God rested from work on the seventh day. As it was God's pattern from the beginning of time, so it should be our pattern too. It is sometimes referred to as a "creation principle" and therefore something much more important than a social or cultural norm.

The concept of Sabbath reinforces the point that we were created to do more than build and produce or to get caught up in the rat-race of life. In our present over-active culture, Christians probably break this commandment more than any other, yet it is the one we rarely comment on when we do. Our attitude to the Ten Commandments is quite inconsistent. For instance, there is enormous community shame around adultery even after there has been heartfelt repentance and true moves towards restoration. Yet, we admire people for not keeping the Sabbath and comment approvingly, "Oh they are so busy!" Some churches commend themselves on their websites by stating, "This is a busy church", as if it were a good thing.

This fourth commandment, to keep the Sabbath, sits as a pivot in the middle of the Ten Commandments. It sits between those which are about how we relate to God and those which are about relating to others. The Sabbath is an antidote to a life governed by too much activity and the expectations of empire. It recentres life on *being* rather than *doing*. It is a chance to taste something of eternity now. It sets limits on economic activity. It affirms it is not right to work all the hours God gives.

The Ten Commandments make it clear that the available time to work is limited; we should not let work "expand to fill the time available". In the economy of Sinai, we are no longer judged by our productivity or financial worth, but rather on how we create and sustain community. Sadly, this is not what empires generally want to hear about.

Egypt and Sinai offer us two contrasting modes of living:

In Egypt it was . . .

With Sinai it was . . .

- Accumulation
- Power (over)
- Exploitation
- Ruled by an elite

- Neighbourliness
- Relationships (alongside)
- Community of collaboration
- Governed through a series of negotiated relationships

In this chapter I have shown God's people left empire on three occasions. First, Abraham was called out of Babylon. He then escaped, by the skin of his teeth, from Egypt. Finally, when the family became a large ethnic community, again in Egypt, they were delivered from brutal oppression and exploitation by the hand of God as the Children of Israel. In the next chapter we will see how Israel found the pull and enticement of empire hard to resist, and eventually gave in.

Questions for discussion

1. How do different people and cultures understand greatness? What does it mean for us, as Christians, to be great today?
2. What are we called from? What are we called to?
3. Do you know of any impressive historical buildings which you suspect, or know, have been built on the backs of the poor?
4. In what ways do we conspire with the belief that the value of our lives is measured by what we do or produce? How do we move from a manic pace of life to one founded on the principles of the Sabbath? Do we strive to try to have it both ways?

Prayer

Lord God,
who calls us to be great
by leading us to another way of living,
help us to find again how the Ten Commandments
can become for us,
not a rod to beat ourselves, or others, with,
but an invitation to be a different sort of people,
free from the demands
of the empires around us.
Amen.

Notes

1. A comparable situation happened during the imprisonment of political prisoners on Robben Island, South Africa in the 1960s. The prisoners were presided over by overbearing white supremacists. During these hard times, the prisoners demanded permission to play football. Every week for three years,

a couple of prisoners would make a request to the governor to play football. It was always refused and often cruelly punished. Eventually the authorities relented. The Makana Football Association was set up and football was played. Through this form of non-violent resistance, the South African authorities began to lose control over the inmates of the infamous prison. To use a phrase of Vaclav Havel, it was an example of the power of the powerless, a principle that Moses understood too. For the whole story see Chuck Korr and Marvin Close, *More Than Just a Game: Football v Apartheid* (Collins, 2009).

2. It is also important today that we should not follow other gods. However, we usually point to other religions as being these "other gods" without realising that we have already sold our souls to the gods of the modern day empires of this age, such as the powerful technology giants Apple and Google, the consumer goods conglomerates Nestlé and Unilever or cultures that depend upon consumeristic and militaristic values. These are dominant within our Western culture and the lives of Christians. I believe these are better parallels to the gods mentioned in the Old Testament, not contemporary world religions.

CHAPTER 2

Israel Chooses Empire

In the previous chapter, I showed how the people of God were seduced by all Egypt had to offer. The great encounter with God at Mount Sinai was meant to be a turning point. Through Moses, God gave the people a charter, the Ten Commandments, for organising the community's life and worship in a quite different way. No longer was exploitation and oppression to play a part in their life. No longer did they have to worship the gods of Egypt which endorsed slavery, greed and misery. No longer were they to be under somebody else's thumb. Now they were with God, who gave them freedom.

It has been said that it took only one day to get Israel out of Egypt, but forty years to get Egypt out of Israel. The mentality and patterns of empire were well ingrained. For forty years, the Children of Israel lived as nomads in the deserts of the Sinai Peninsula. They carried with them the precious Ten Commandments in a large, ornate box made of rare woods: the Ark of the Covenant. This "in-between time" in the wilderness, before getting to the Promised Land, was an opportunity to form God's new way of being and living. Eventually, though, their time of wandering came to an end and Moses passed the baton of leadership on to Joshua. They were now to become settlers in the land that Abraham had also made his home.

On entering Canaan, Israel lived as a confederation of tribes based on the Ten Commandments. There was no hierarchical or centralised structure of government. They did not follow the dominative patterns of empire, have a king, or an emperor. They had God. They also had a succession of judges, both men and women, who helped them negotiate how to live as a generous community across the twelve tribes and obey the law. Their priests led them in worship of the God who brought them liberation. The ways of empire were not to play any part in the life of Israel.

However, in time, the people looked at the countries around them and saw that they had kings who ruled with all the paraphernalia of monarchy. These kingdoms seemed strong and attractive with their armies and wealth. Israel decided they wanted what they had. The people started to turn their backs on God by breaking the tenth commandment, "You shall not covet" (Exod. 20:17).

Israel demands a king

After a couple of hundred years living in the hill country of Canaan, the cry was heard, "We want a king like the other nations." Israel wanted to be a power like those around them—Babylon, Egypt and the other smaller kingdom states. God warned the people of the consequences if they adopted the ways of empire in Israel. Samuel was told, "You shall solemnly warn them, and show them the ways of the king who shall reign over them" (1 Sam. 8:4–18).

> The king will take the nation's sons into his army.
> He will make them work in the arms trade to manufacture weapons of war and in the fields to provide food for his army.
> Young women will be taken into his palaces to carry out domestic chores and probably for sexual services too.
> The king will take the best of the agricultural land . . .
> . . . 10 per cent of the grain.
> . . . your slaves and the best of your animals.
> . . . and your livestock (8:11–17).

Samuel concludes, "In that day you will cry out because of the king you have chosen . . ." (8:18). Yet, despite these frightening warnings, the people were adamant they should have a king so "we also might be like the other nations" (8:19–20). The shift from Sinai back to empire was therefore initiated by the will of the people.

Saul

A young man called Saul, the type of man most mothers would be happy for their daughters to marry, was chosen as Israel's first king. He appeared to have many of the natural attributes required of a leader. He was tall, good-looking and had been successful in battle, which impressed the people. As a charismatic leader, the people believed he could save them from the threats they faced, especially the Philistines. He was, though, very spirited and somewhat unstable.

To his credit, he made little or no attempt to transform the tribal structure of Israel into a centralised state, which the kings who followed him did. Saul did not impose taxes or force conscription into the army. However, he was seduced by the gods of the nations around Israel and, when he felt threatened from within the nation, he slaughtered the priests of God (1 Sam. 22). Ultimately, Saul turned out to be too unpredictable and was a disaster. He lacked the profound insight and wisdom of Samuel the prophet.

David

David was chosen as the next king of Israel. His beginning looked more hopeful. He was not the obvious choice, though, being the youngest and least significant of eight brothers. Initially, David had a heart for God and sought to rule as God would have him rule. Nevertheless, in his reign we start to see significant change from the leadership of the judges to a centralised state where power is invested in the king. From a confederation of tribes, Israel was finally and fatefully manipulated into an empire based on the model of the "other nations" that surrounded it.

King David became the ruler of an empire-state which eventually stretched from Lebanon in the north to the border with Egypt in the south. Israel was at the peak of its political and military power. Even while David was just the anointed heir to the throne, the women of Israel sang a song that included the line, "Saul has killed his thousands, and David his tens of thousands" (1 Sam. 18:7). David was the first king in Israel to act as commander-in-chief of the army. To consolidate power in the monarchy in Jerusalem, he gathered around him a group of courtiers and so started to establish his chosen elite. These were the special class of men referred to as "servants of the king", who enabled David to establish control over the people. As a result, Israel rapidly became like the other local empires.

Jerusalem became the focus of this power, where the heart of the nation's faith was established. David brought to the city the Ark of the Covenant, which ironically, contained the Ten Commandments; the principles of how Israel should live differently. He had an ambition to build a stone temple for God but had to be content with the continued use of the mobile tabernacle of the wilderness period—the option favoured by Nathan, the prophet, and probably by God too. This tent-based temple was a wonderful icon of the anti-imperial spirit which God wanted his people to nurture.

To weaken the tribal confederation further, David took a census of all the people of Israel. From this, he was able to impose taxation, begin military conscription and establish work camps of forced labourers (2 Sam. 24). So forceful was the grab for power initiated by David that, at the end of his reign, his sons were engaged in a violent competition to inherit the throne and succeed their father.

David's initial popularity began to decline as the people started to resent the way he had taken the power from the local tribes to himself in Jerusalem. At the end of his life, David was a pathetic and depressed figure who died while his family fought over his poisoned legacy. His final instruction to Solomon, the son who would succeed him, was:

> I am about to go the way of all the earth. Be strong,
> be courageous, and keep the charge of the Lord your
> God, walking in his ways and keeping his statutes, his

> commandments, his ordinances, and his testimonies, as
> it is written in the law of Moses, so that you may prosper
> in all that you do and wherever you turn. (1 Kgs 2:2–3)

David never stuck to this instruction himself. Did he realise his mistake
on his deathbed? We will never know. Solomon also ignored the law of
Moses and continued to build and develop the institutions of an imperial
state that God had never wanted. As a result of David's reign, another
terrible shift in the direction of Israel's journey had been taken. Empire
was now firmly established in Israel and it was set to get worse.

Solomon (1 Kings 1–11)

We like to have strong and wonderful leaders. Maybe it is because we feel
they will deliver us from what makes us anxious. King Solomon is usually
cast in such a role. He is regarded as the wise king because of the judgment
he made in a dispute by two women over a baby. He built a stone temple
where God could reside at the heart of Israel. He sought to make the
country strong and was admired by foreigners. Solomon was associated
with wealth and opulence, reaching heights of riches that other kings of
Israel could only dream of. Those close to him enjoyed dazzling material
prosperity. However, this only tells part of the story of what transpired.

Solomon was not the eldest son of David and, therefore, not the legal
heir to the throne. Adonijah, his half-brother, was. Nonetheless, through
family intrigue and infighting, Solomon won the crown. In order to
consolidate his position and to remove any possibility of dissent, Solomon
had Adonijah executed soon after he became king. Thus Solomon's rule
did not even start in the spirit of Sinai. It started with murder.

He continued as he started. Throughout his reign, he ruled as a despot,
apparently not caring for the previous confederation of the twelve tribes.
By nature he was ambitious and selfish. To increase and magnify his own
glory, he gathered to himself immense power and possessions: gold,
precious items, armies of horses and chariots (the same deadly weapons

Egypt attempted to use against the Children of Israel as they escaped slavery), together with a thousand wives and concubines. He used slave labour on an enormous scale to complete his grand building projects. He imposed a heavy burden of taxation on the people to fund these. He centralised all power round himself, moved worship to Jerusalem and scorned the local holy places dotted around the countryside.

In Solomon, we see how true Jesus' comment is that you cannot serve God and mammon. You will choose one or the other. Solomon broke the commandments in great style by choosing ever-increasing wealth and power. He did not choose God.

The Old Testament tells us four times that Solomon was Pharaoh's son-in-law. He had, as it were, "married the boss's daughter". Through this relationship, the values of empire from Egypt penetrated deep into the heart of Israel, right to the place where God should have been reigning as king. In Solomon we see classic imperial behaviour. He became a "Pharaoh in Israel" who gathered much wealth and power to himself at the expense of the ordinary people. Solomon implemented the policies of Egypt in Israel. The Old Testament theologian Walter Brueggemann ruefully reflects, "It was as if the Exodus never happened."

In summing up his life, the book of Kings states it plainly: "God was angry with Solomon" (1 Kgs 11:9). He had let his heart follow the gods of empire.

The kings

I believe God always thought Israel would end up opting to have a king. The passage in Deuteronomy 17:14–20 indicates this. The sense of it is:

> If and when you get a king (as you probably will), he should not have many horses or wives, otherwise his heart will be turned away from God; he must not gather to himself gold or silver in great quantities. When he takes his throne, he should have this very statement with him at all times. He

should read it every day, and his main job is to make sure that he fulfils it. Furthermore, he is no higher in status than any other member of the community.

I like the following African investiture hymn for a new king. It feels so much closer to the anti-empire spirit. Solomon would never have allowed it.

> You are a turd,
> You are a heap of refuse,
> You have come to kill us,
> You have come to save us.

The kings completely ignored Deuteronomy 17 (the instruction to live as a modest king) while also ignoring the prophets. The prophets continually pointed out injustice and idolatry in Israel and the imperial mind-set it produced. They said the whole royal edifice, built on covetousness and greed, would eventually come tumbling down—and it did.

If the legacy that David left Solomon was poisoned, what Solomon left to those who followed him was much worse. The rot had truly set in. His kingdom split into factions. There were rifts within his family and civil war broke out. Like so many dominant leaders, when Solomon was taken out of the equation, what remained simply fell apart. The nation split into two kingdoms. The northern kingdom called Israel and ruled by Jeroboam was based on ten of the original twelve tribes. The southern kingdom called Judah and ruled by Rehoboam was based on the tribes of Judah and Benjamin. Events continued to spin wildly out of control.

Samuel's warnings had come true. The nations' sons were taken into the army and embroiled in the arms trade, young women were taken into the kings' palaces and the people were taxed heavily. They were exploited and lost their power. In short, God's alternative way of living had been rejected and the people were enslaved once again. Israel sang that God was king, but in reality this was not true. The construction of Solomon's amazing buildings in Jerusalem did nothing to reduce the anger and resentment of the people, which had really started to set in during the reign of David. It was never God's intention that Israel should become great like the "other nations". It was God's plan that he should be king and shape Israel to become a great nation—as God understood greatness, based on the Ten Commandments. However, the kings themselves tried to make greatness happen by following the ways of empire. We all face this temptation.

There were two kings, however, who stood out from the others: Hezekiah and Josiah. Hezekiah had something of a mixed track record. In one report, we learn that he did what was right in the eyes of the Lord (2 Kgs 18:3–7). He tore down the pagan centres of worship and destroyed artefacts which honoured the gods of the surrounding empires. We learn he kept the commandments given by God to Moses. He refused to toe the line with the king of Assyria, making it clear he would not serve him. He had drawn a line in the sand.

However, we also have another report (2 Kgs 18:13–16). Here, we are told that when Assyria attacked Judah, Hezekiah changed his mind: "I have done wrong; whatever you impose on me I will bear." In order to pay off the king of Assyria, he gave him all the silver of the temple and the gold that overlaid the great doors and their posts. These two reports suggest that, while Hezekiah wanted to do the right thing by God, the practical difficulties of following this through overcame him. He wanted to resist empire, but also wanted to maintain the security of the nation. He must have felt he was between a rock and a hard place.

Of all the kings, Josiah had the best reputation and track record. As a young king in his twenties, he initiated a great programme of reform in Judah, part of which was to refurbish the temple. During the building work, "the book of the law" was unearthed. On reading this, Josiah was greatly alarmed because it spelled out what the consequences would be if its instructions were not obeyed. Consequently, he ordered a public reading of the scroll in Jerusalem for all the people to hear. He also renewed the relationship agreement which had been established between God and his people when the Ten Commandments were first received.

Next, he set out to rid Judah of other nations' gods, religion and worship which the people had taken on board. He promoted the exclusive worship of God and outlawed worship of any other kind. Finally, he reinstated the Passover festival that had not been celebrated since before the time of the kings. This festival, of course, was the great liturgy which celebrated their freedom from the oppression and exploitation of empire—the Egyptian empire. This was a clear sign that Josiah understood what God required if they were not to be like "the other nations".

However, there was also a dark side to Josiah. He was extremely violent when he put an end to the worship of other gods from outside Judah. Even so, he was highly praised by the writer of the book of Kings (2 Kgs 22:2; 23:25) and by the prophet Jeremiah because "he judged the cause of the poor and needy" (Jer. 22:6).

Apart from a few, the kings of Israel were not the least bit interested in what had happened at Sinai. Instead, they sought to be great by the measure of those around them, and so chose to expand and consolidate their power and wealth. They ruled with absolute power in a highly patriarchal society. If people felt the oppression of the monarchy, then women were doubly troubled as they also suffered the oppression of men. There was a deadly interconnectedness between patriarchy and empire. It is only when Jesus came that there was any hope of women being treated differently.

The prophets

Prophets were those who spoke for God, but unlike the priests or court officials, they were rarely establishment people. In a sense, they were the conscience of the nation, often having to confront the King and his inner circle. When nations acted like empires, they sought, or even assumed, approval from God for what they have already decided to do and the manner in which they wielded power. The prophets were the brave women and men who stood up to this power and named what was wrong. Their role was not so much to see into the future, although this did sometimes happen; instead they were those who could see clearly what was already happening in the present. They were, more often than not, people of insight rather than foresight. They sensed what they believed to be the voice of God and then boldly spoke it.

These extraordinary people were advocates of the diverse and varied communities which made up Israel. They were people of Sinai and the

Ten Commandments. They believed the uncompromising God of Israel was also the true king of all people and all nations. They were anti-empire people and were vocal about it. It is therefore not surprising they came into conflict with the powers-that-be as they confronted the kings and their cronies—those with vested interests.

Being a prophet was a dangerous vocation. They were often rejected, and even at times executed, by the very people to whom they were trying to communicate God's word. People who enjoy power, position and prestige rarely like being told they have got something wrong.

The prophets also brought new life to God's people when they were at their lowest point of defeat in exile. Prophets could see possibilities for a new future as they were (to use a phrase of Walter Brueggemann's) people of "Hopeful Imagination". It was not that they could tell in detail the specifics of the future, but they could see God still had something to do for his people. They could sense the shape and spirit of what this might look like. We now turn to look at two such prophets.

Isaiah

The early chapters of the book which bears the prophet's name concern a time when the southern kingdom was threatened by its powerful neighbour, the empire of Assyria. The prophet, though, saw that the real threat to the life of the nation was not the might of their overbearing neighbour, but Judah's own structural and endemic injustice.

Isaiah 5:8–23 denounces the evil of social injustice within the community. Throughout the passage, a word is repeated which is often translated as "woe". The NRSV translation of the Bible represents it as "ah".[1] The word is not so much a threat against the people as God revealing his sadness about a people he loved. Their life and culture was in decline because they were travelling the wrong way.

The prophet talks of rich and powerful people who live as if they were people of empire. They buy up all the land and property so that there is no room left for anybody else:

> Ah, you who join house to house,
> who add field to field,
> until there is room for no one but you,
> and you are left to live alone
> in the midst of the land! (5:8)

These are the people who no longer need to work for a living because they profit from the labour of others. As a result, they drink all day:

> Ah, you who rise early in the morning
> in pursuit of strong drink,
> who linger in the evening
> to be inflamed by wine. (5:11)

God is also distressed because they employ euphemisms to cover up their ways, calling evil good, and good evil. They switch the meaning of the words "light" and "darkness", and "sweet" and "bitter", to benefit themselves while all the time the poor suffer:

> Ah, you who call evil good
> and good evil,
> who put darkness for light
> and light for darkness,
> who put bitter for sweet
> and sweet for bitter! (5:20)

This is not why God called Abraham out of Babylon or rescued his people from Egypt. The prophet speaks for God and denounces the injustices of the rich.

This pattern continues today. We live in an economy where we have not only joined house to house and field to field, but also bank to bank, shop to shop, factory to factory, and business to business at the expense of the small trader. Many of us have benefited financially from these arrangements. However, if one walks onto some urban estates across our country, it is clear there are many people who have not fared well under this financially-driven system. The message to those who have grown so rich is "Woe to you, you'd better look out!" Eventually big trouble came to Jerusalem's economy because it had become greedy and acquisitive, and it had destroyed the concept of neighbourhood. When financial collapse came, it tasted like "sour grapes". It seems as if big trouble has come on us today as our economies have attempted to squeeze too much from the poor through sub-prime loans and by relying on playing the financial markets. It is not that God is out to get us; it is simply what happens, sadly, when we live in ways which do not embrace God's neighbourly way of living. They are the natural consequences of the wrong way.

Like the people Isaiah was addressing, we employ euphemisms to cover up what we would rather deny, or not acknowledge. Instances of double-speak from recent history include:

- "The Final Solution to the Jewish Question" meant "the death camps of Hitler";
- "Little Boy" was the name given to the atomic bomb that was dropped on Hiroshima;
- "Peacekeeper" was a land-based intercontinental, multiple-headed, nuclear ballistic missile;
- "Operation Iraqi Freedom" meant "War on Iraq";
- "Collateral damage" means "the death of innocent people".

To live this way is to contravene how God wants the world to work and is unsustainable.

Amos

Our second example is Amos. He addressed the northern kingdom, Israel, during a period of great prosperity and religious piety, when there was comfort and security. That said, Amos saw this prosperity, built on injustice, was limited to a small number of people; it was accumulated by oppressing those at the bottom of society. He proclaimed Israel would be judged for its insincere worship along with its evil injustice.

We have that sorrowful word again, translated here as "Alas":

> Alas for those who lie on beds of ivory,
>   and lounge on their couches,
> and eat lambs from the flock,
>   and calves from the stall;
> who sing idle songs to the sound of the harp,
>   and like David improvise on instruments of music;
> who drink wine from bowls,
>   and anoint themselves with the finest oils,
>   but are not grieved over the ruin of Joseph!
> Therefore they shall now be the first to go into exile,
>   and the revelry of the loungers shall pass away. (6:4–7)

In these verses, the prophet addressed the privileged class who had such great wealth they could afford to lounge around on the most luxurious beds imaginable, made from ivory, and feast on lambs and calves. Only the mega-rich could afford to take the young from their flocks of sheep and cattle for food. The poor had to let their animals grow into maturity if they were to make the most of them economically. These idle people also sang meaningless songs. They had become wrapped up in trivialities and ignored those they made their wealth from. Amos is clear: these people will be the first to go into exile.

Exile

The date 587 BC is deeply etched in the history of the people of the Old Testament. This was the year when the Babylonian armies overran Jerusalem and destroyed everything. While it was clearly a military and cultural defeat, it was also regarded as God running out of patience with his people; his sorrow turning to anger.

The city was totally devastated and the kingdom therefore came to an abrupt end. The ruling elite and wealthy landowners were carried off into exile in Babylon. The seriousness and enormity of this defeat cannot be overstated. The only parallel for us would be if the Soviet Union had invaded Britain during the Cold War and destroyed everything that was important to us and our way of life.

What Judah lost . . .	Would have been as if Britain had lost . . .
▪ All governance	▪ The Houses of Parliament
▪ The Temple	▪ St Paul's and Canterbury cathedrals
▪ The monarchy	▪ Buckingham Palace and Downing Street
▪ The economy	▪ The London Stock Exchange and the banks
▪ The rule of law	▪ The law courts and the police force

It is hard for us to understand what this defeat felt like. When the ruling elite of Jerusalem arrived in Babylon, after a long journey of transportation, they would have been blown away by what they saw: an amazingly powerful nation with its life carefully planned to impress and intimidate. Babylon was a magnificent and sophisticated imperial city which had many astounding public spaces. Its buildings were the largest and most wonderful on earth. It included the stunning Hanging Gardens. It was a city designed to make other capitals (such as Jerusalem) look like backwaters in comparison. It was full of opportunity and oppression.

Here in this foreign land, some yearned for home and sang Psalm 137: "By the rivers of Babylon—there we sat down and there we wept when we remembered Zion." (In time, this yearning moved them to rediscover their past, the story of God and the story of the way out of empire, rather than the way into it.)

There was no bigger shock God's people could have faced. It looked as if exile was the end of everything for them. It stripped away the complacency and security Israel took for granted. They seemed to have believed God's patience was eternally elastic and his anger was just a continual background warning noise. Finally, though, it seemed as if God had had enough and declared, "If you want empire that much, then you can have it in all of its fullness", allowing them to be taken into Babylonian captivity. In today's terms, we would call this experience of defeat a "critical incident"; a situation that causes us to re-evaluate everything and make choices about how we might proceed differently from this point onwards.

The people had to ask the crucial question: "How could God have let this happen to us?" Painful and humiliating though exile was, it started to lead them back to God and to newness.

Empires today

It is easy to see the Old Testament story purely as an interesting history lesson, as if empires were a thing of the past. It suits us to take this view, as we do not want to see ourselves as being embroiled in injustice and oppression. We want to be seen as freedom-loving people who spread good values throughout the world, rather than colluding with enslaving elements within it.

It would also be easy to begin naming empires of our time as being "over there". But this is a dangerous game, as it allows us to point at others and distance our own, often unintended, allegiance to oppression. As I have already said, empires are not only nations, they are any power which has the resources to usurp other's energy, demand their cooperation and loyalty, and oppress.

God is not against nations. God is not against large companies or organisations. God is not against mass movements. God is against self-serving systems or groupings of people that seek to lead others deeper into enslavement, exploitation and domination. God's passion is strongly anti-imperial because of the tremendous suffering it produces. God's story is about leading people out of enslavement into freedom with him, with each other and in harmony with all creation. It is only in this we can find the foundation for our wealth, security and well-being.

Questions for discussion

1. Empires of today are not just based on nations. See how many of today's empires you can name (consider financial institutions, political movements, family or tribal groupings, religious organisations and other everyday networks and associations that people join).
2. In what ways do these control or influence our lives? Is there anything they might do which would cause us to disassociate ourselves from them?
3. Does this chapter change our view of some of the traditional Biblical heroes?

Prayer

Oh sorrowful God,
>who looks on our ways of ordering life
>with pity and anger.
May we recognise our tendency
>to follow the ways of empire,
and why the injustice it causes
>provokes you to wrath;
for the sake of the oppressed,
>for our sake
>and for your sake.
Amen.

Notes

1. The New Revised Standard Version (NRSV) of the Bible is an English translation released in 1989.

CHAPTER 3

This is What Empires Do

Empires come in many shapes, sizes, guises and styles. Our contemporary empires are sometimes more difficult to detect than the imperial nation states of the past. Yet today's empires influence and control so many aspects of our lives without us realising, unless we stop to think about it.

While not every nation, corporation or organisational structure acts like an empire, most tend to. It is as if groups of people with any degree of power have a default setting they cannot help but move towards. This in time becomes a major flaw, if we allow it. (This happens, of course, on an individual level too. We keep returning to wrong habits and patterns of behaviour and we wonder whether we will ever change. It should not be a great surprise when it occurs at the communal and corporate level too.) It does not have to be this way, but sadly we are seduced into following the way of the big, the better, the impressive, the successful and the powerful. It is a hard temptation to resist.

In this chapter, we are going to take a detour away from the story of the Old Testament to look at some of the characteristics and traits of empire.

We do not realise how deeply the spirit of empire becomes engrained in us. As a small boy I was unconsciously inducted into the mind-set which regarded some things as having a higher rank or status than others. I was fascinated by cars. In my vast collection of models made by Corgi, Dinky and Matchbox, there was a strict pecking order. I knew which cars were the "posh" ones, and which were not. My favourite ones were generally those that powerful or rich people drove. As a six-year-old, I had already been inducted into an understanding of prestige in the motor trade.

In a variety of ways we have all been subtly inducted into the spirit of empire. Again, I will use the example of motor cars. Most people understand the importance of hierarchy among the different brands of cars on our roads: we have vehicles made by Skoda, Rolls-Royce, Jaguar, Hyundai, Kia and Mercedes-Benz. If you want to demonstrate your status and look important on the road, then many people would know you should drive a Rolls-Royce, Jaguar or Mercedes-Benz. While Skoda, Hyundai and Kia produce reliable, comfortable and decent cars, they do not convey prestige in the same way. This is an example of the imperial mind-set at work.

There is, of course, nothing wrong with having a smart car for a wedding or other great event. However, I believe it becomes contrary to God's way when we feel the need to reinforce our status or impress on other people our image, wealth or rank in life through the things we own. I have used the brands of cars here to illustrate my point. I could have easily used another product, such as designer clothes, tableware or wristwatches.

In the spirit of empire, we want to be part of something that is highly regarded and seen as successful—and therefore powerful. By following this way, we are enticed away from God's alternative path for life.

Regardless of their name, size, or structure, empires often share many traits and tendencies. Here are some of the more common ones.

Empires gather wealth to the centre

The first trait of empire is acquisitiveness. A simpler word is greed. Empires tend to gather to themselves, over time, money (capital) and land (resources). This wealth is not shared equally among all who participate in the activity of the empire; for instance, its workers and customers. It ends up in the hands of just a few—an elite. This happened during the reigns of David and Solomon where the "servants of the king", the courtiers, benefitted greatly from the wealth of the nation because of the assistance they gave to the king's imperial ambitions. This wealth was, of course, created by those who worked the land, but who nevertheless ended up poor.

Desmond Tutu, the former Archbishop of South Africa, is reputed to have remarked, "When the missionaries came to Africa, they had the Bible and we had the land. They said, 'Let us close our eyes and pray.' When we opened them, we had the Bible and they had the land."

The transfer of wealth from the many to the few occurs through a variety of mechanisms: biased tax policies; the withdrawal of profits; the imposition of high interest rates on loans; monopolising a market; increasing land ownership or simply direct military intervention. Once this movement of wealth gets established it gathers a momentum all of its own. The rich get ever richer and more powerful, and the poor become even more destitute. I think this is what Jesus may have meant when he said, "For to those who have, more will be given; and from those who have nothing, even what they have will be taken away" (Mark 4:25). We, however, usually spiritualise this saying, removing its sting and power; we say it refers to faith rather than wealth.

Eventually the rich become so prosperous they do not have to work any longer: a lifestyle condemned by the Old Testament prophets. Mahatma Gandhi endorsed the message of the prophets when he listed "wealth without work" as the first of his deadly sins. This is not God's way.

Empires restrict power to the few

This second trait is closely related to the first. Ordinary people, small people, are not given access to power. True power is kept in the hands of the king, the dictator, the major shareholders, the wealthy and the well-connected. There may well be an illusion of consultation or democracy to create an impression everyone has a part to play. Ultimately, though, a small minority of people hold all the cards. They make the best of their networks to consolidate their position. We see this today when a small number of people use their family ties, private clubs, university connections and business interests to enhance their privilege. They hold onto their advantage in life and, at one level, I cannot blame them—but this is not how God wants it to be. This is not in the spirit of Sinai.

Eventually, and predictably, empires decline and fall. This can be the result of the small, controlling elite over-stretching itself, or simply through complacency and arrogance. Then, the whole imperial edifice starts to come tumbling down. The falls of dictatorships illustrate this very well.

Empires impose uniformity

It suits imperial organisations if variety and diversity are reduced as much as possible. They are then able to exert more control and operate more efficiently, to their own financial benefit. Sadly, the effect of this can be devastating for the life of local communities and their cultures. This approach resists other forms of creativity which do not originate at the centre. Creativity from the edges is unwanted as it is unpredictable and therefore uncontrollable. Diversity and difference, and all the gifts they bring, are discouraged. Empires require conformity and compliance—but God is the God of diversity and difference.

Imperial nations usually insist their language is used by their colonies in the affairs of government and commerce. As a result, European languages have spread all around the world in the wake of the empires. Mark Tulley, the long-time BBC India correspondent, speaks of English as being a "killer language" in the Indian sub-continent because of all the regional languages it has squeezed out.

Uniformity is also seen in the fast food and retail industries. Their global outlets are designed so that customers have a similar "customer experience" wherever they go. Clothes stores have the same feel about them and often identical products. This sameness reduces variety and marginalises local preferences and traditions. The tendency to uniformity is also seen in the computer and software business. Up until recently, it was estimated 90 per cent of the world's desktop and laptop computers were running Microsoft Windows operating systems, although this dominance is now being eroded by people's increasing reliance upon mobile devices.[1]

The argument for uniformity often sounds very reasonable because it is more practical and efficient, and therefore economical. In the process, however, much is lost from local communities and cultures. Here in Britain, we regularly hear the moan that every high street looks just the same nowadays, as all they consist of the same retail chains.

Through uniformity, empires are able to manipulate, control and exploit markets, and the communities they purport to serve.

Empires use violence to impose and maintain control

Through the battles and wars of Saul, David and Solomon, the kingdom of Israel was founded on violence. Regrettably today, Israel is again embroiled in violence. The expansion of all empires inevitably relies on violence. The British Empire relied on the force of arms. One terrible example happened in 1919 at Amritsar, India. All public meetings were banned for fear of an uprising. When the local Brigadier-General heard 20,000 people had gathered for a meeting in one of the city's gardens, he dispatched his troops to the scene. On arrival, he ordered his men to shoot into the crowd. They kept firing on the crowd for almost ten minutes, by which time most of their ammunition had run out. Hundreds of men, women and children were killed, and untold numbers injured.

Saddam Hussein imposed control in Iraq through terror and violence, as does Robert Mugabe in Zimbabwe. The House of Saud employs the same tactics in Saudi Arabia. The business of empire is a nasty one.

Not all violence is physical. It can be economic. Cheap goods can be dumped on vulnerable markets so any competition is eliminated. Dirty tricks, campaigns or other unfair practices are employed to get a trading advantage over other companies. Local shops find it impossible to continue in business when a few supermarkets become so dominant in the market.

When I was in Macclesfield, the retail giant Tesco wanted to build one of its "Extra" megastores near to the town centre. It was feared that many small and local traders on the high street would be threatened or put out of business by such a development. After a long "No to Tesco" campaign in the town, the big retailer backed down. A mega-store was a step too far. Many people have similar feelings about the domination of Amazon, and other global players, with the impact this has on booksellers and other retail outlets. These large corporations are not concerned for the welfare of Macclesfield, or any town for that matter, except for where this serves their own interests. A corporation's primary concern is its share price and the dividend it pays out. This is enshrined in law in Britain: companies must put these priorities before anything else. Ultimately, empires serve themselves and no one else, and often they use bully-boy tactics.

Violence and oppression are also used to maintain control. It is not easy being a king, an emperor, a CEO or a major shareholder of a dominant business. The fear is that somebody may usurp your position or advantage in the nation or the market. Emperors do not sleep well at night. They never feel secure no matter how much they have. In fact, the more they have, the more insecure they usually feel. In the days of Joseph, Pharaoh had a dream (Gen. 41:1–36), as Nebuchadnezzar did in the days of Daniel (Dan. 2:1–45). These were not pleasant sweet dreams, however. They made them scared: they were nightmares. An emperor's most powerful instinct is to use all of the might at their disposal to keep things as safe and secure as possible for themselves. Thus, all forms of violence are used against any threat which is perceived to have potential to bring down the empire and upset the status quo.

Empires do not value local cultures

Empires have over-inflated ideas about their own importance and sophistication. They somehow believe they are essential to others' development and even to their survival. To appear superior though, somebody else has to look inferior. This dynamic was seen when European nations colonised parts of Africa and Asia. Native historians tell us that the attitude of colonising powers was that local people had no history worth considering or acknowledging. European history was taught in schools without regard to African history just as the English language was taught without regard to local native dialects. This devaluing of local culture only served to perpetuate existing patterns of domination. The Congo was called "Darkest Africa" and regarded as dangerous, savage, untamed and uncivilised. Many of these places were invaded for the resources which could be exploited and not appreciated or valued for what they already were.

One of my favourite sayings from the time of the British Empire comes from Gandhi when he visited Britain. He was asked, "What do you think of civilisation in the West?" (you can detect the superior, imperial attitude in the question). Gandhi was no fool, though. He answered, "I think it would be a good idea."

Local cultures and traditions are belittled, treated as unimportant, or worse, patronised as being a quaint curiosity. It is as if they have not progressed "like we have". What indigenous communities value is viewed as immature, simple and childish. They are not taken seriously. As local and native cultures are side-lined, so are their people.

It is easy to see how an attitude develops that regards these "backward" cultures as in need of improvement by "us, a more sophisticated people". Even worse, these local expressions can be excluded and eliminated as being worthless. The irony is that the empires were reliant on the labour and cooperation of these local cultures and communities in order to exploit the raw materials needed to feed their expansionist aspirations.

A sad comment, which illustrates this tendency to belittle local cultures, was made at a Christian group studying Islam in Birmingham. The largest local ethnic group in the neighbourhood had its origins in Kashmir, Pakistan. A Christian lady of many years' standing, and involved in church leadership, exclaimed in her frustration over the local population, "But they're still wearing pyjamas!", referring to the traditional shalwar kameez clothing which most of them would wear. Fortunately, she has since moved on, but I fear the attitude has travelled with her.

Empires make use of symbols and logos to reinforce their imperial message

Walk into any shop and you are bombarded by images and logos plastered across products and promotional material. The use of symbols is nothing new, especially in the promotion of political power or corporate interests. Throughout history, regimes, movements and commercial ventures have used visual techniques to impress in societies' minds their dominance and doctrines. Dictatorships place images of the leader in public places all around the country, reinforcing in people's minds who is in control. As in most imperial systems, images of the Emperor were a common sight throughout the Roman Empire during the time of Jesus. Images of Caesar were found in most public places: in the market square, public baths, theatres and temples. They could be found on personal items and, of course, engraved on the coinage (Matt. 22.20–21).

Companies today spend vast amounts of money perfecting their corporate identity and making sure they are regularly seen by the public on products, billboards and in the media. We were given a party game one Christmas, called The Logo Board Game. It draws on what we know about the different corporations we encounter on the high street and on the web, asking questions about their products and seeing if we can recognise their company symbols. Through a party game, the empires have further invaded our lives to reinforce their corporate messages.

Brands, with their symbols and logos, sometimes carry even more weight than the products themselves. We can look again at the motor industry for an example of this. In 1998, the high-class car manufacturer, Bentley Motors, was bought by Volkswagen, the volume car producer. Some parts of the British brand are developed and made by the German parent company. However, if the badges which identified the vehicle as a Bentley were removed and replaced with the "VW" of Volkswagen, sales would drop. This is because people are not just buying a car, they are purchasing an image (or an experience, as the advertisers would have us believe). "Bentley" carries greater prestige than "VW".

Adults and young people are duped into buying clothes that have a company's logo emblazoned across them (e.g. Nike, Adidas, Fat Face). Children at school will fall out over these brands as some are considered "cool" and others not. We pay good money for these labels and, in the process, provide the clothing companies with free advertising.

National identities are frequently represented by the symbols of animals, and they each reinforce a message of strength or power. This was true even in the days of the Old Testament. Then, the eagle represented Babylon, the bear represented Medea, the leopard represented Persia, and the iron-toothed beast represented Macedonia. I will leave you to work out for yourself which of today's nations use the following images of animals to represent them: the eagle, the bear, the lion and the dragon.

We have a God though, who asks us not to make images to represent him. His presence is all we need.

Empires co-opt religion to make their violence look respectable

History shows us that nation-empires often believe they have a God-given right to behave as they do. In war, people pray to God as if God is on their side, just as the enemy prays a similar prayer. National leaders believe they are fulfilling the will of God by making war on those who live differently to them and hold different values, even if it means innocent people (including children) get caught in the "collateral damage" that ensues. Both George W. Bush and Tony Blair felt their pursuit of the 2003 war in Iraq was something God would have them do, or had even called them to do. They clearly viewed themselves on the side of good against evil even though we, as Western nations, are historically complicit in the troubles of the world, especially in the Middle East.

Sadly, there are too many examples of religion being used to support or condone military violence.

During the second Iraq war, when the allied troops entered Baghdad, a communion service was held on the Sunday for the troops. The Anglican chaplain who led the worship said, "This week we have seen resurrection," as if overwhelming military force could bring the transformation we read about in the Gospels.

In 1981, the American Navy launched a nuclear-powered attack submarine that was named "USS *City of Corpus Christi*", after the American city. "Corpus Christi" literally means, the "body of Christ". More recently in Britain, in 2007, the Bishop of Carlisle led a service at the Barrow-in-Furness shipyard at which he blessed the nuclear-powered submarine HMS *Astute*, equipped with advanced cruise missiles, when it was launched. The first of these submarines was given a sacred name, the second was given the blessing of the church.

At the Queen's 2012 Diamond Jubilee celebrations, a thanksgiving service was held at St Paul's Cathedral. Then, a little later, there was a fly-past of military aircraft over Buckingham Palace, including an example of the Lancaster bomber which was responsible for the deaths of over 60,000 innocent people in the Second World War. This was a weapon of mass destruction.

You may well ask if I am proposing we should all be pacifists. Despite the endurance of the just war theory over so many centuries, we do not seem to be able to get past the fact that Jesus never condoned violence. His kingdom was, and is, non-violent. Martin Luther King Jr held onto this principle through the Civil Rights campaign, even though he knew it would probably cost him his life. Unfortunately, in 2012, we spent $1.76 trillion globally on the development of warfare but a much smaller amount on the United Nation's Millennium Development Goals.[2] We may or may not be called to be pacifists, but we are called to be non-violent. This does not necessarily mean, though, that we should sit back and do nothing. Indeed, the Bible calls us to take action. At times we may need to be outspoken and practice peaceful resistance, even subverting the status quo.

Imperial leaders like to believe they bring peace through violence—but we have to face the fact that this is not what Jesus taught. For him, peace comes through suffering love. This is the opposite of empire.

Empires increase inequality

Equality and fairness among people is toxic to empire; they prefer to nurture inequality. Such inequality destroys community and collaborative ways of working. Open conversations and the sharing of resources disable imperial ways of working as the effectiveness of their command and control systems is eroded. It is amazing, but not surprising, that in God's way of doing things, with greater equality, everybody is generally better off. Empires seem blind to this.

In 2010 a fascinating book was published by two British academic epidemiologists, *The Spirit Level*.[3] It is the result of a 30-year-long study on the patterns, causes, and effects of health and disease conditions in populations. It concludes that more people are happier and healthier when there is less difference between the rich and poor. As inequality increases in a society, the following problems become more serious and severe: obesity, teenage pregnancy, violence and crime, oppression of women, educational performance, imprisonment, social mobility, mental health, community life and social relations difficulties, life expectancy and homicide.

Interestingly, this study demonstrates that in some of these categories both rich and poor people are worse off in highly unequal societies. This is true, for instance, of life expectancy. If societies are more equal, everybody has a better chance of living a longer life. Even the small elite will, on average, live a longer, more healthy and happy life. However, poor people are worse off under all the above categories when there is a great disparity in wealth.

The spirit of empire is about power *over* others and *over* the created order. This is in contrast to God, whose way is in cooperation *with* people and *with* creation. These trends and traits of empire are typical of structures, nations and organisations which seek to gain power and control rather than those that seek to share it and collaborate with others.

Questions for discussion

1. Which minority cultures are not valued today? The gap between rich and poor has widened over the past decade. Why do you think this has happened?
2. List what you think are the top ten brands which dominate our lives today. "We want to be part of something that is highly regarded and seen as successful—and therefore powerful." Why is this?
3. What examples have you seen where religion and the military have been uncomfortably close?
4. Where have you seen uniformity imposed which has reduced the richness of life?

Prayer

We are boxed in,
hedged in, and surrounded
by many powerful corporations,
  familiar brands and glittering logos
  that demand our attention
  and allegiance.
Help us to trust
that this is not the only way to live,
  and that those who shout the loudest,
  or who have the most enticing advertising campaigns
  are not usually choosing God's better way.
Help us to follow the humble way of Sinai
  and the kingdom of God,
  today and every day.
Amen.

Notes

1. <http://nr.news-republic.com/Web/ArticleWeb.aspx?regionid=4&articl eid=25931901>.

2. When the Millennium Development Goals were initially set by the United Nations, the World Bank estimated that the foreign aid required to reach the targets by 2015 was only between $40–60 billion a year.

3. Richard Wilkinson and Kate Pickett, *The Spirit Level: Why Equality is Better for Everyone* (Penguin, 2010).

CHAPTER 4

Keeping Empire out of Israel

God's people discovered that living obediently, according to the Ten Commandments rather than by the oppressive rules of Egypt, did not come easily. Even when the Children of Israel had been in the desert just a short time, they felt drawn to return to Egypt and abandon the plan of God. The old ways of empire had their comforts: food and shelter were two obvious ones. This urge to return must have felt something like the pull an alcoholic experiences when drawn back to the bottle. To go back to it offers so much relief—in the short term. When in the wilderness, Egypt looked enticing and seductive.

Living the imperial way has been compared to an addiction. We know from history it is a way of life which does not ultimately work as all empires eventually collapse and fail. Yet we keep going back to it—this is a form of insanity. The Twelve Step Programme of Alcoholics Anonymous defines insanity as doing the same thing over and over again expecting a different result.

A problem with any economic system, even if people are not greedy and selfish, is that some people do better than others. This can happen simply because some people get "lucky breaks". I once came across a local man who used to be a lowly sales representative for a chain of food shops. Over time he was promoted up through the company until he became the sales director. He had done quite well and so had the shops. However, the company eventually went through a bad patch when the economic climate deteriorated and the owners decided to sell the business. After a few meetings together, the directors decided to take the bold step of buying the business themselves. They mortgaged their homes to raise the capital and the deal was done. A couple of years passed and the fortunes of the business turned around and its profits increased rapidly. Eventually, they decided to sell the chain of shops, cash in their shares and retire as the economic situation has recovered. By his mid-forties, this acquaintance of mine had amassed several million pounds in his bank account, bought a very nice house and one of the largest off-road vehicles I had seen in a long time. He said to me in amazement, "I've never seen so much money!" In some senses, he felt that he just happened to be in the right place at the right time. He had had his lucky break.

Many of us in the West are much wealthier than so many others in the world, simply by accident of birth. We happen to have grown up in one of the richest nations on earth. This is our lucky break. Having this advantage we tend to hold on to our wealth. It gives us power.

God does not seem to have a problem with wealthy people as such. Indeed, he expects those who have much to care for those who have little or nothing. What I believe God does have a problem with, though, is our attachment to what we have and our mistaken belief we cannot live without it.

As Israel was prone to take the journey back into the empire way of living, institutions and structures developed in Israel favoured the powerful and rich, and not the poor. The rich were then (wrongly) regarded as the ones who had God's blessing which further consolidated their position as the leading elite of the nation.

As a result, one of the crucial issues Israel had to address was this: how do you stop some sections of the community getting a permanent economic advantage over others? How should the community prevent some families or tribes becoming permanently better off, while others never got an opportunity to improve their economic situation? In the books of Leviticus and Deuteronomy, there are instructions and laws on how to deal with this.

We know the Ten Commandments are central to Israel's call to live differently to Egypt. However, they are very brief and general, rather than detailed. They do not tell the people how to live in their specific situations. Because of this, each generation has had to figure out how to apply the Ten Commandments in their own particular context. There was a lively debate about how they should be implemented and obeyed in Jesus' day.

We too have to work out how they apply in a post-industrial, digital age, as the Bible does not address this specifically.

In the books of Leviticus and Deuteronomy we have texts which attest to Israel's attempt to define what it would mean to live by the Ten Commandments in their situation. They specify how worship should be carried out, how to deal with sick people, how to treat slaves and what to do about marriage break-up, etc. They also address the matter of inequalities in wealth and how to maintain economic justice in the community.

You may not know, but Deuteronomy 5:6–21 is a near identical repetition of the list of commandments in Exodus 20:1–12. In this restatement it is interesting to note the commandment about the Sabbath has been expanded and reinforced:

> Observe the sabbath day and keep it holy, as the Lord your God commanded you. For six days you shall labour and do all your work. But the seventh day is a sabbath to the Lord your God; you shall not do any work—you, or your son or your daughter, or your male or female slave, or your ox or your donkey, or any of your livestock, or the resident alien in your towns, so that your male and female slave may rest as well as you. Remember that you were a slave in the land of Egypt, and the Lord your God brought you out from there with a mighty hand and an outstretched arm; therefore the Lord your God commanded you to keep the sabbath day. (Deut. 5:12–15)

This version of the fourth commandment has inserted the reminder again, "Remember that you were a slave in the land of Egypt." This was a fact Israel must never forget.

As they travelled together through the wilderness away from Egypt, God's intention was that Israel's journey out of empire should be a permanent one. Their purpose was not to enter the Promised Land to set up an empire of their own in rebellion against Egypt. Instead, they were heading to Canaan to live with each other and with God in a totally different style of society, which would demonstrate to all the nations how to be true communities. They were to be a light to the Gentiles.

Here below are four of the chief instructions they were to follow. They each have their roots in the Sabbath principle, which was at the core of God's revelation to Moses at Sinai. Their purpose was to keep the ways of empire out of Israel. They were contrary to the ways of Egypt and they are contrary to today's dominant global economics.

Cancel all debts every seven years (Deuteronomy 15:1)

This first instruction is an elaboration of the Sabbath commandment. It states that every seven years (i.e. on the Sabbath of years) all debts should be cancelled. Loans could last no longer than seven years. When the Sabbath year came, the debtor was free from his obligation to repay the loan. This encouraged responsible lending and borrowing. It was a natural limiter on irresponsible lending. Long-term indebtedness to other people is one sure way to sink into poverty from which it is hard to recover. Later on we will encounter Jesus dealing with the social reality of debt in the Gospels.

There have been repeated calls since before the millennium for the Western nations to cancel the debts of the poorer nations in the same spirit. Some work has been done, but there is still much more to do.

Liberate all slaves every seven years (Deuteronomy 15:12)

The second instruction as part of this vision was that no one should have to serve as a slave any longer than seven years. Again, this Sabbath year brings a benefit for those who are in a less powerful position in the community.

This rule meant every enslaved person had a chance to be free again and play a full part in society and the economy. It also meant there would no longer be a class of people who were forever designated as the underclass. In addition to this, when slaves were set free, there was an obligation on their owner not to send them away empty-handed. They had to be generous towards them by giving them sheep, corn and wine so they had a chance to make a new start and not fall back into slavery again.

In amongst this, God reminds them yet again of the path they have travelled, "Remember that you were a slave in the land of Egypt, and the LORD your God redeemed you; for this reason I lay this command upon you today" (Deut.15:15). The implication being, "If I did not choose to free you, you would still be slaves in Egypt. So you too should choose to free others."

Let the fields lie fallow every seventh year (Leviticus 25:1–7)

The third part of this vision is that the land should also enjoy a Sabbath year. We have continually exploited the environment for our own ends. We see ourselves as the masters and the earth as our servant or slave. Israel had to let the land have one rest year in every seven to remind the people they did not own the earth; they were only stewards of it. In this seventh year, there was to be no harvesting of the fields or the vineyards. The source of food for that year was only to be what the earth naturally produced. The land was to have a chance to renew its life.

Redistribute the land every fifty years (Leviticus 25:13)

To ensure no long-term structural injustices set in, Jubilee was established. This was to be the year after a "Sabbath of Sabbaths" year (i.e. $(7 \times 7) + 1 = 50$). Every fiftieth year was to be this special Jubilee year. In this year, everyone had to return back to the land their family was originally allotted.

It was like pressing a giant "reset" button. Doing this gave the whole community the chance to start afresh and stopped the poor becoming eternally poor.

The redistribution of the land was to remind people again that everything belonged to God, not to them. This is how God's economy works, not that the rich like it. The Jubilee process prevented systemic injustice developing and stopped the wealthy thinking they were some sort of special elite chosen by God, above other (poorer) people. This is a revolutionary way of looking at the distribution of capital and undermines our assumptions about how the economy should work today. This is probably the most dangerous economic teaching in the whole Bible.

Today's Jubilee Debt Campaign is inspired by this ancient principle. The campaign calls for a world where debt is no longer used as a form of power by which the rich exploit the poor. It is part of a global movement which demands freedom for all those who suffer from the slavery of unjust debts. It demands there should be new financial systems that put people first.

Put caring and generous practices in place (Deuteronomy 23–24)

Not only do we have the principles of Sabbath being worked out in community relationships and the economy; there are also directions in the book of Deuteronomy which pay attention to those who will not even benefit from these. The people were instructed:

> Do not charge each other interest. (23:19)

> Do not take collateral on loans. (24:10)

> Do not withhold payment of wages from poor people. (24:15)

When you reap your harvest of olives, grapes and grain[1], leave some behind for the orphan, the widow and the immigrant. (24:19–21)

Yet again, this passage ends by telling Israel why they should do this: "Remember that you were a slave in the land of Egypt; therefore I am commanding you to do this" (Deut. 24:22). All through the book of Deuteronomy this reminder is repeated to impress on the people how hard it was in slavery and that God's ways are different.

The New Testament and Jubilee

People ask if this radical redistribution of land happened very much during the Old Testament period. We do not know exactly. We do know that Jesus took Jubilee seriously. He did not just see it as a nice metaphor; it was at the heart of his ministry. The early believers continued this tradition.

Jesus spoke about the year of Jubilee at the beginning of his ministry in a passage which is sometimes referred to as his "manifesto statement" (Luke 4:18–19). He proclaimed "good news to the poor", together with "release for captives" (i.e. slaves). He announced "the year of the Lord's favour", a phrase picked up from Isaiah (Isa. 61:1–2), which refers back to the Jubilee principle established in the book of Leviticus. By proclaiming Jubilee, Jesus was teaching that debts should be cancelled and slaves should be freed every seven years. He was affirming the land should be fairly redistributed once a lifetime. This was definitely good news to the poor.

We shall see later there were very strong echoes of Jubilee when the Spirit came at Pentecost. As its name suggests, the feast of Pentecost is the fiftieth day after the feast of Passover. It is the time when Jubilee is remembered and reinforced in the mind of Israel.

Walter Brueggemann tells of a practical example of a banker attempting to live by the principles of Sabbath:

A concrete embodiment of the Jubilee commandment was evidenced in a rural church in Iowa during a "farm crises". The banker in the town held mortgages on many farms. The banker and the farmers belonged to the same church. The banker could have foreclosed. He did not because, he said, "These are my neighbours and I want to live here a long time." He extended the loans and did not collect the interest that was rightly his. The pastor concluded, "He was practising the law of the Jubilee year, and he did not even know it." The pastor might also have noted that the reason the banker could not take such action is that his bank was a rare exception. It was locally and independently owned, not controlled by a larger Chicago banking system.[2]

The final word goes to Desmond Tutu, a vehement campaigner for the cancellation of the debts of the poorer nations: "I've called for a long time for the cancellation of the crippling debt, which we have had to bear for so long . . . this is the new moral crusade: to have the debt cancelled, following the Biblical principle of Jubilee. Basically, this principle says everything belongs to God; all debts must be cancelled . . . to give debtors a chance to make a new beginning."

Questions for discussion

1. What do you feel about people who have worked equally as hard as you, yet have ended up much poorer? How can you get a better idea of what it feels like to be trapped in poverty? Are there some ways in which you can share your life with them more often?

2. Have you had "lucky breaks" in your life which have contributed to your wealth? Have you had "unlucky times" in your life that have left you poorer than others?

3. Why do we find it almost impossible in our churches to talk about what our personal or household income is, and what capital we

have tied up in property, investments and pensions? How might we overcome this?

4. Look at the Jubilee Debt Campaign website: <http://www.jubileedebt.org.uk>. Is there something on it that can help you, or your church, engage with the issues of debt that cripples the lives of so many people?

Prayer

May God bless us with discomfort . . .
at easy answers, half-truths,
   and superficial relationships,
so that we may live deep within our hearts.
May God bless us with anger . . .
at injustice, oppression,
and exploitation of people,
so that we may work for justice, freedom, and peace.
May God bless us with tears . . .
to shed for those who suffer from pain,
   rejection, starvation and war,
so that we may reach out our hands to comfort them
and to turn their pain into joy.
And may God bless us with enough foolishness . . .
to believe that we can make a difference in this world,
so that we can do
   what others claim cannot be done.
Amen.

A Franciscan Benediction, source unknown

Notes

1. These were the three main cash crops.
2. Walter Brueggemann, *Finally Comes the Prophet: Daring Speech for Proclamation* (Fortress Press, 1989), p. 104.

CHAPTER 5

Early Genesis Stories While in Exile

We started our journey through the Old Testament with Abraham. It is now time to look at some of the stories from the very beginning of the book of Genesis. These really became Israel's stories during the time of their Babylonian captivity—their exile.

As I have previously said, the year of Jerusalem's defeat, 587 BC, was completely devastating for the people of God. Everything was lost. A large proportion of the population was forcibly removed to Babylon. It included people of influence in the spiritual and economic life of the city together with the ruling elite. These people are usually referred to as the "exiles". An even larger proportion of the people were left behind, however. Their experience was also one of exile. Everything that gave them their sense of identity and purpose had been ripped from them. The city and the land had been left desolate. They too were no longer "at home", even though they remained in the same place. They too were dominated by the Babylonian imperial way of life. They too felt as though God had abandoned them.

There is no getting away from the fact that when the exiles arrived in Babylon, they encountered an impressive civilisation and highly developed culture. This was not what they had expected.

As they settled in Babylon, with Jerusalem lost and their God apparently impotent, they had to figure out how to live as Jews in this strange place—but it is hard to work anything out when you have been severely humiliated. As a result, far away from home, national depression set in. They had always presumed God would come and deliver them, as had been the case on numerous occasions previously. Their grief was unbearable.

All they could do was to bewail and lament what had happened to them and all they had lost. This was their cry:

> How we are ruined!
>> We are utterly shamed,
> because we have left the Lord,
>> because they have cast down our dwellings (Jer. 9:19)

The prophets also felt this pain of loss:

> The Lord has forgotten me,
>> my Lord has forgotten me. (Isa. 49:14)

It is significant that in addition to the people and the prophets, God also felt pain. He did not come away unscathed:

> Look away from me,
>> let me weep tears of bitterness
> do not try to comfort me
>> for the destruction of my beloved people. (Isa. 22:4)

The same sort of grief was expressed by Jesus when he foresaw Jerusalem would be defeated and its people scattered once again:

> Jerusalem, Jerusalem, the city that kills the prophets and stones those who are sent to it! How often have I desired to gather your children together as a hen gathers her brood under her wings, and you were not willing! (Matt. 23:37)

This was yet another instance when Jerusalem refused to take the non-imperial path, the way of the kingdom of God, as Jesus would call it.

When loss and grief have done their worst, there is usually a moment when some newness is envisaged or imagined. There comes a moment of hope, where hope is the belief that God has still got something to do. This is quite different to optimism, which is the tendency to expect the best possible outcome in a situation. Hope believes that one day, God will act.

In difficult times, when despair has been sapped of its energy and bitterness has no longer any place to go, the possibility of a different future starts to emerge. It was in just such a situation, when all light had been extinguished for the exiles, that God raised up individuals who would resist the lure and temptations of empire while in exile. These were the prophets.

Thus, in a place where all seemed lost, great things began to happen. The Israelites eventually started to make the significant move from having a religion based on a temple, to having a faith rooted in a text. They became the people of the book.

It was during this period of tragedy and crisis that much of the Old Testament was discovered, remembered, written, compiled and edited. The Jews were forced to ask some searching questions of themselves and of God:

- Why had God, who was supposed to be almighty, allowed such terrible things to happen to his people?
- What stories should they now tell their children, the Babylonian ones or those of Abraham, Isaac and Jacob?
- What songs should they sing now they were no longer in Jerusalem?

They could not get away from hearing the stories of Babylon with their imperial messages. The city and its culture continually retold the stories and reinforced their messages. It seemed as if the Babylonian gods were in control of everything, including the future—but God's people knew these were not their stories. They had to dig deeply in an attempt to reconnect with God. In doing this, they uncovered many of their own old stories which told something radically different to the ones which echoed along the streets of Babylon. These, from their past, told them about a God who reigned over all the gods and empires of the world.

Before we look at a selection of these found in the early chapters of Genesis, we will look at one of the most important Babylonian narratives.

The Babylonian creation story *(Enuma Elish)*

According to the Babylonians, in the beginning there were two gods—Apsu and his wife Tiamet. They had plenty of children ("god-children") who made a lot of noise, preventing Apsu and Tiamet from getting a good night's sleep. Irritated and frustrated from their lack of rest, Apsu and Tiamet decided to murder their children. However, one of the younger gods, Ea, heard of the plan and before his parents could act, killed his father Apsu. Not too long after this, Tiamet got herself another husband, Kingu. Full of anger, she was now a formidable force and planned her revenge.

The god-children held a conference to decide what they could do. They chose Marduk, another of the children, to kill their mother. But he wanted a reward for carrying out such a daring assignment. He asked for his own palace to live in and a city to go with it. It was agreed. Marduk attacked his mother, and being younger and fitter, "ripped her body apart like a clamshell". From this gory mess all the animals and living things which covered the earth were created.

As agreed, Babylon, together with a marvellous palace, was then built for Marduk—but after a while he wondered who would keep his palace and the city clean for him and his fellow gods. New creatures would have to be made for this. Marduk then killed Kingu and used his blood to fashion these new servants of the gods, and so human beings were made.

This story tells us that the city, the empire and the society of Babylon were all rooted in violence; that creation came into being as a result of bloodshed, destruction and murder. This was the story God's people heard in exile—but it was not their story.

Just as we revisit, each year, a number of key Bible stories at our annual festivals, the Babylonians retold and re-enacted their stories of empire, like Enuma Elish, at their ancient version of the school assembly, mystery play or crib service. From these stories they drew their values, beliefs and behaviours. Their creation story told of the victory over chaos by means of violence. They believed the gods favour those who conquer and shed blood. They believed any problem faced by an individual or the state can be, and probably should be, resolved by hitting back and destroying the enemy once and for all. This view is still dominant today. On it rests the belief that peace can be achieved through violence. The theologian and activist Walter Wink has entitled this view "The Myth of Redemptive Violence". He writes:

> No other religious system has even remotely rivalled the myth of redemptive violence in its ability to catechise its young so totally. From the earliest age, children are awash in depictions of violence as the ultimate solution to human conflicts. Nor does saturation in the myth end with the close of adolescence. There is no rite of passage from adolescent to adult status in the national cult of violence, but rather a years-long assimilation to adult television and movie fare. Not all shows for children or adults are based on violence, of course. Reality is far more complex than the simplicities of this myth, and maturer minds will demand more subtle, nuanced, complex presentations. But the basic structure of the combat myth underlies the pap to which a great many adults turn in order to escape the harsher realities of their everyday lives: spy thrillers, westerns, cop shows, and combat programmes. It is as if we must watch so much "redemptive" violence to reassure ourselves, against the deluge of facts to the contrary in our actual day-to-day lives, that reality really is that simple.[1]

As the exiles were overwhelmed by their experience of the great city, so too were they overwhelmed by this Babylonian story. They, like us, found it hard to believe violence did not win at the end of the day. Back in Jerusalem, they had exalted their kings who had defeated foreign armies and eradicated any dissent by force. Now, in Babylon, some of them realised they had been following the wrong story.

In the face of all of this, God's people had to ask what story should they tell their children if they were not to be assimilated into the ways of Babylon. When they asked this question, they discovered the answer was to retell their foundational stories. These confirmed the Babylonian stories were not theirs. They had a markedly different creation story which gave them identity, security and partnership with God.

In the first eleven chapters of Genesis we have five important stories: the first creation account; the second creation account and the Garden of Eden; Cain and Abel; the Flood; and the Tower of Babel. What matters in these stories is not whether they are true or not, but what they mean for those in exile. We will now look at three of these.

The first creation story (Genesis 1:1–2:3)

The creation account at the start of the book of Genesis differs from the Babylonian creation story in almost every respect. There is no violence. There are no divisions in creation; no part of it is outside of God's concern or control. God takes the chaos and transforms it into something generous and beautiful; something which does not have to be feared.

This would not have made any sense to the Babylonians. For them, everything outside their creation (city and empire) was wild and dangerous. It was evil; it was to be feared. The only way to remove this threat would be by conquering and subduing it. Peace could only be established and maintained through violence. This is not so in this Genesis account of creation.

In Genesis 1, each day of creation is an act of love, beauty and wonder. It is a work of transformation where chaos is changed into fruitfulness and fear into trust. The God of Israel is the one who brings life and wellbeing. To crushed and defeated exiles, it declared God was the Lord of all life. It was the good news they desperately needed to hear.

Day 1: Light is created and God declares that it is all good.

Day 2: Water and sky are formed out of the indistinct mass of material.

Day 3: Land takes shape with vegetation and plants. It is not formed from violence. It is not wild or dangerous. God declares that it is all good.

Day 4: Sun, moon and stars are created for light and to contrast the day and the night. God declares that it all is good.

Day 5: Living creatures arrive on the scene. God, again, declares that it is all good.

Day 6: Animals and people take their place in the foreground of creation. God declares that it is all good. And then the text is audacious when it says that humans are created "in the image of God". Finally, it says that God saw it all and declared that it was *very* good.

God's declaration of his works as "good" is an important counterpoint to Babylonian creation stories. Humans are not servants of dominating and oppressive gods. We are created in the image of God. He calls us to become cocreators with him in his ongoing work of creation. This is partnership.

Day 7: God rests on the seventh day. At the end of six working days, God stops to enjoy companionship and rest.

There are two points to note about the passage here. First, when our Bibles translate the original Hebrew word *tav* as "good", they do not really do it justice. In our culture, "good" could be taken to mean merely satisfactory, or simply "okay". The Hebrew word carries with it the sense of creation being full, delightful, fat, incredible and wonderful. It is a gift to be embraced and enjoyed which is so unlike the universe understood by the Babylonians—a universe which is to be feared. God's creation drips with goodness.

The second point to note is the idea of Sabbath is key to this first creation story, just as it is to the commandments of Sinai and the Jubilee principle. For Old Testament people, the Sabbath day was one way of living a God-centred life and, therefore, an anti-imperial life. They believed that to keep the Sabbath was to be like God, as this is what God did after the six days of creation. More than enough was made in six days so it could be enjoyed on the seventh. God is not a workaholic.

I used to believe the crown and pinnacle of all creation was when human beings were made. Now, as I read the text, I see the climax as being the amazing gift of Sabbath rest. Babylon never offered this. Neither do empires today.

The inclusion of the Sabbath into our way of life is probably the most important mark of our identity as God's people, yet it is the one we find hardest to keep. It does not primarily exist so we can attend church, but so we can stop working. It is a weekly opportunity to take time out from producing and consuming, selling and buying, achieving and acquiring, which is what empire wants us to do. Empire always wants us to work more, do more, earn more, have more, spend more, eat more, and possess more. The Sabbath reflects that what we "have" and all we "do" in six days is more than enough. It puts a "limiter" on us. We do not have to work every hour God gives. It is important to note, though, that we do not rest one day a week so we can work even harder on Monday either. The Sabbath is a sign we belong to God because, being in his image, we behave as God does. It is also a sign that time belongs to God.

The Sabbath represents the stopping of all the activity which empire wants us to continue doing. It is our chance to find, once again, who we are and who we belong to. It is a time to receive life. It is an opportunity to enjoy community and relationships, and nurture one's spirit.

Digital technology has brought us many great benefits, but it is not without its darker side. Computers and communication devices urge us to be on the go all the time, to work 24/7. They are switched on all day so we are always "on call", sending and receiving messages. We constantly text, tweet and the like, which make us worry more about all the things we believe need to be done. This is just one example of how empire can distort good gifts so they end up becoming a curse to us.

For exiled people in the chaos and confusion of empire, the creation story reminded the Jews that God could bring order out of chaos and replace violence with goodness. It taught people how the Sabbath could restore their life and hope, and help them resist the power of empire.

The second creation story and the Garden of Eden (Genesis 2:4–3:24)

The second creation account ends with what is commonly called "the Fall". Most Christians have grown up with an interpretation which goes as follows: Adam and Eve were placed in the idyllic Garden of Eden. They enjoyed each other's company, enjoyed God's company and had everything they needed. In the middle of the garden were two special trees: the "tree of life" and "the tree of the knowledge of good and evil". The latter was to become their downfall. This was the only tree they were commanded not to eat from, but they did. It ruined their relationship with each other and they started to be scared of God. Because of what they did, they were expelled from Eden. Then, they had to graft and toil to survive. They suffered struggle and pain as they cultivated the land and in childbirth. Through their disobedience, Adam and Eve allowed a fault-line to enter the human heart and all creation. As a result of their rebellion against God's instruction, sin entered the world.

This, however, is only one way of looking at the passage. It is an interpretation which goes all the way back to St Augustine, around the year 400 AD. However, all of the stories of the Bible are multilayered in their meaning and application. The incident in the Garden of Eden can be understood and applied in more than one way.

One of the difficulties I have had with the traditional interpretation of the Fall, since my childhood, is the prohibition to eat from the tree of knowledge of good and evil. Surely, one would think this would be a good fruit to eat. It would help us live a good life and make right choices. However, God says that, "In the day you eat of it you shall die" (Gen. 2:17). How can this be so? Did God give a random command not to eat of this tree simply to see if Adam and Eve could obey instructions? Was the tree there just as a test? I do not think so. Here, then, is another way of looking at this passage.

There was a time when humanity lived and walked with God. This is symbolised by Adam and Eve at peace in Eden. The instruction not to eat of the tree of the knowledge of good and evil is the first sin warned against in the entire Bible: it is therefore a very important matter. Eating from the tree leads to death, whereas not to eat of it is lifegiving. Those who eat of the tree do not become wise (as one might guess); they become preoccupied with what is good and what is evil; by what is true and what is false. They become consumed by who is right and who is wrong; who is on our side and who is not. It is a search for control which needs answers, explanations and resolution. It is not a search for love.

To eat of this particular tree is to live a life that divides the world into "goodies" (ourselves) and "baddies" (everyone else). The result of eating of this fruit is that you really believe you know what is good and what is evil. You then make judgments over others and end up having to "watch your back" as those you make judgments about may well retaliate. When you live this way it is no longer a life of harmony, unity and peace. In eating of the tree, Adam and Eve found they lost the paradise they had so enjoyed. The world became a dangerous place to fear.

God says we should not go round dividing up the world into a world of our friends and enemies, of those we like and those we dislike; of the included and the excluded. Jesus was very clear on this point: "Do not judge, so that you may not be judged" (Matt. 7:1). In his ministry he embraced the excluded and opposed those who promoted a divided world. He called us to love our enemies as well as our neighbours. In saying this he removed the categories of enemy and neighbour, of them and us. The mind-set of empire though, is to divide, set against and fear the other. It is a way of living which is preoccupied with control, where some are regarded as our friends (those we can live and work with) and others labelled as enemies (those we will not live and work with).

To make judgments over others is to act as God. At the end of the account God declares, "See, the man has become like one of us" (Gen. 3:22). We will soon see a similar complaint arises in the story of the Tower of Babel. Before Adam and Eve are cast out of Eden, we learn God shows compassion to them. He comes and covers their shame by clothing them (Gen. 3:21).

I believe this story does not tell God's people they have simply done bad and naughty things or that they have broken some arbitrary rule. It tells them they have chosen the imperial way of "divide and rule". They did not choose God's other way, which brings unity to everything. This story is also our story. We also make similar choices; all that is different is the setting. This is an archetypical Jewish story which speaks across generations. It is still important today.

The Tower of Babel (Genesis 11:1–9)

Our third story is about an imperial building project: the Tower of Babel. At first, it looks to be the result of good and great human endeavour. In fact, it was another example of not living according to God's instruction.

At the end of the first creation account, humans were commanded, "Be fruitful, multiply and fill the earth" (Gen. 1:28). This very same instruction was repeated when God made his covenant with Noah following the flood (Gen. 9:1). Prior to the Babel story, we know the generations following Noah spread themselves "in their lands, with their own language, by their families, in their nations" (Gen. 10:5, 20, 31). Even though they spread themselves out, they remained one interrelated people. By doing this they fulfilled their divine purpose and the stage was set for the wellbeing of the whole of creation.

However, when we come to the account of the Tower of Babel, the mood changes dramatically. The people are now scared at being scattered across the face of the earth (Gen. 11:4). They resist God's purpose for creation and devise their own plan. They migrate to one place to build a city based on a massive tower.

This is fortress mentality. It is the mentality which says it is better to stick together where there is safety in numbers and with people who live similar lives. It prefers self-sufficiency, autonomy and homogeneity. It rejects diversity, interrelatedness and trust in God. To make their fortress tower they have to make bricks (Gen. 11:3).

Bear in mind this is a story to help exiles make sense of their situation. The memory of brickmaking will remind them of their ancestors in Egypt making bricks for Pharaoh's imperial buildings. When they heard this tale about Babel, they would have realised what making bricks is all about—slavery, exploitation and misery. Still, today, wherever there are great imperial projects, there are always small people "making bricks", or the equivalent.

As I write, news is breaking about the appalling cost of India's brickmaking industry. The country's booming construction sector relies on the output of two million brick workers. Many, including children, are bonded labourers working in conditions of near slavery, earning, at best, £1.50 for a twelve-hour day.

There is also abuse and exploitation in other manufacturing sectors. In April 2013, a large textile factory collapsed in Bangladesh killing over one thousand people. It was known to be unsafe and the workers received very poor wages. The "race to the bottom" for the cheapest clothes in our shops here in the West means corners are cut. There is always a social cost to the imperial urge to "get ahead" and build up more wealth in ever-growing industries.

What, then, did the people of Babel fear if they allowed themselves to be scattered? The text indicates they feared they would be nobodies. So they came together "to make a name for ourselves" (Gen. 11:4). They had one language. They built an enormous tower city. They were creating for themselves what we might call a "collective ego" (a theme we shall return to later on). They were concerned they should look good in other people's eyes. They were trying to create a sense of being impressive and in charge of their own destiny. Here, we see the faulty human impulse to build up, centralise and monopolise in order to gain control and feel mighty. This story is about empire, and more specifically for the exiles, the Babylonian empire. The tower at Babel mirrored the Ziggurat tower cities of the empire the Jews now found themselves in. Babylon, like Egypt, was built on the wrong premise and on the backs of the poor.

In the account, God came down to see this tower where everybody spoke the one "superior" imperial language and where other cultures had been marginalised. At Babel, they had established a monoculture. This was never God's plan or intention for humanity; diversity was. At Babel, the lust for power and dominance had become unstoppable, or would have been until someone put a stop to it. This is why God came down and ended it. The one language, which was very efficient for economic activity and made it easier to manipulate a population, was broken down into many and the people were scattered over the face of the earth. This is not so much a punishment for being an arrogant people, but more importantly, God re-establishing the way things should be.

Part of the fault line through humanity causes us to prefer uniformity. This is not how the universe is though, because God loves difference. Yet, the temptation to sameness and building up power and wealth in one place is enormous. It makes us feel good, significant and strong. But it does so at the expense of so many other people. It resists God's design for variety, difference and complementarity; we end up putting ourselves in the place of God. As human beings, we are made in the image of God, but we are not God.

We will see, when we look at the New Testament, that Pentecost becomes the antidote for Babel and empire as it embraces the diversity of languages and peoples, and the Sabbath principle of Jubilee.

Questions for discussion

1. How would you explain the "Myth of Redemptive Violence" to a friend who shares your faith? Do you think violence can bring true peace? Do you think Jesus thought violence could bring peace?

2. How can you best use a Sabbath day so you enjoy your relationships, nurture your spirit and avoid, as far as possible, buying and selling with the large companies which dominate our country?

3. The church in Western nations has been in numerical decline for a long time now. Do you ever experience feelings of loss about this? Do we have something in common with the exiles when they experienced loss when taken from Jerusalem?

4. Fairtrade is about better prices, decent working conditions, local sustainability, and fair terms of trade for farmers and workers in the developing world. Take a look at their website: <http://www.fairtrade.org.uk>. Should we buy goods made in the Far East which we suspect have been made with very cheap labour?

5. Do you recognise our impulse to build up and centralise? How can this destroy diversity and variety? How can we promote diversity and variety?

Prayer

O God of all the nations,
we are fearful people.
We do not trust
    that it is enough to belong to you.
So we build up impressive things around us:
    buildings, structures, congregations
    and achievements.
We do not believe
    that what we have in you is sufficient.
Teach us how to value
    the small,
    the different,
    the vulnerable,
    and all that challenges what we have already.
Teach us how not to always seek
    to build up,
    have more,
    or appear stronger.
Because
    this is what Jesus was like,
    this is what you are like,
and as we are made in your image,
this is what we should be like.
Amen.

Notes

1.   Henry French (ed.), *Walter Wink: Collected Readings by Walter Wink* (Fortress Press, 2013), p. 156.

CHAPTER 6

Empire and the Inner Life

We are now going to make our second detour from the texts of the Old Testament. The material in this chapter may, on first reading, seem to be somewhat tangential to the main theme of empire we have been following—but it is not. Here, I will explain that what happens with groups of people (societies, corporations and nations) also happens within the heart of the individual. The two aspects are inextricably linked by the fault-line that runs through all humanity. What affects us as we live and work together also affects us in our personal lives.

The temptation that communities face to follow the way of empire, rather than God's alternative way, is also the pull each person knows in their own heart and soul. What is common to both of these is the "False Self". To grow into maturity as individuals or groups of people, we must deal with the power and place of identity in our lives. We have to become people of compassion, generosity and willingness, rather than what the False Self wants us to be: competitive, fearful and wilful.

Each person has to deal with their individual identity and a corporate entity has to deal with its collective identity. The spirit of empire is simply the collective identity of a society, business, church or nation. It has a need to control more and have more; a need to be right and have status. War happens between nations when one collective identity fights another; when neither is prepared to give way to the other. Empires and False Selves are interested in power over others, not shared life and love.

As individuals, each of us carries a burden. The majority of us, most of the time, find our personal existence hard to bear. We constantly look around to find ways to ease this burden. A common way we do this is to associate with a group: a club, a denomination or church, a point of view or a cause. Doing this, we feel more significant; we find a sense of purpose and our loneliness is reduced. This is okay as far as it goes. But, sadly, we find it easier to belong to a group than to belong to God. To know we belong to God, and to find all we need is in God, is at the heart of true prayer.

In the New Testament, Jesus rebuked Martha in the home she shared with her sister Mary (Luke 10:41–42). She was moaning about Mary who chose to sit at his feet instead of helping with getting the lunch ready. Jesus said to her, "Martha, Martha, you are worried and distracted by many things; there is need of only one thing. Mary has chosen the better part, which will not be taken away from her." While it is important to make sure the family is fed, there is no more important spiritual pursuit than to find who it is we belong to. Mary knew this. If we do not know who we belong to, then we do not know who we truly are.

Sabbath

Probably more than anyone else, Thomas Merton has helped Western Christians rediscover the contemplative aspect of prayer.[1] It dawned on him that we had become people who lived on the circumference of our lives, with little or no access to our inner selves. In fact, he would go further and say many people do not think there is anything within us; there is only what is on the circumference. Because of this, we have become people who are not centred (literally, "eccentric"). How then do we reconnect with our inner lives? Prayer, as silence, is key to this.

Silence is related to Sabbath. When the law was given to Moses at Sinai, as God's other way, the principles of rest and Sabbath were placed at the heart of the community. It is crucial to take time out from "business as usual" for ourselves. Our 24/7 world demands we are on the go all the time, doing this, that and the other. Forming patterns of silence in our lives is essential if we are going to live in an anti-imperial way. We need to take time to live more deeply. To live more deeply does not require a more complicated and busy prayer life, though, but a life where there is simplicity and space.

In the BBC TV series, *The Big Silence*, where five people with quite different backgrounds explored contemplative prayer, Abbot Christopher Jamison guided them with these excellent words: "Silence is the gateway to the soul, and the soul is the gateway to God." The best things in life cannot be described through language or words; they are far beyond them. Love, of course, is chief among these things.

We suffer from a glut of information. So much is available to us now, especially in the age of the Internet, that we are inundated with the noise of words. We need contemplation and silence today probably more than at any other time in our history, yet Sabbath rest is more elusive than ever.

When we do take days off we find it hard to simply rest. Rabbi Abraham Heschel, one of the leading Jewish theologians of the twentieth century, advocated lives deeply rooted in rest. He said:

> Sabbath is not an occasion for diversion or frivolity; not
> a day to shoot fireworks or to turn somersaults, but an
> opportunity to mend our tattered lives; to collect rather
> than dissipate time.[2]

It should not become a rod for our backs with rigid regulations about what is permissible and what is not. As Jesus said, "Sabbath was made for humankind, not humankind for the Sabbath" (Mark 2:27). We must find new ways of establishing the silence of Sabbath for the sake of our inner lives, for the sake of community and for our collective sanity. If not, we are in grave danger of gaining the whole wide world while losing our souls.

Busyness

Not only do we suffer from a lack of silence; we have also crammed our lives full with activity. We have become overly busy people. This has happened without us realising it. When I was a child I remember we were promised in the decades to come there would be increasingly more leisure time with reducing working hours. The big question was what we would do with all this time. Now we have to ask ourselves, what went so wrong? How did we get this busy? To make it worse, we have even made a virtue out of it.

I am often asked, "Have you had a busy week?" If I say, "No, I haven't", I feel as though I have not been pulling my weight and doing my bit; after all, those asking me the question are busy! We suffer from a terrible disease where we are all expected to be on the go most of the time. This is not a Sabbath lifestyle.

This busyness has become a mark of importance and significance today. Friends will tell you with pride how busy they have been. We somehow feel we are more important and worthy if we are doing a thousand and one things without a minute to spare. Couples bringing up children tell me they are like ships passing in the night. This is disastrous. We are wrecking what is most important to us by not taking Sabbath into our lives.

I was recently on sabbatical leave (despite all the sins and weaknesses of the Church of England, I am so glad it still allows its clergy to take this time for rest and renewal once in a while). Being relieved of Sunday duties, my wife and I went along to other churches. At one morning service, following the theme of the Epiphany, was communion. It included simple music, poetry and a minimum of liturgy and speaking (brevity seems to be their motto). It was all over in forty minutes. It was wonderfully refreshing and uplifting. Before the morning was out, we were back at home, calm and relaxed, drinking coffee and thinking this is what Sabbath should *really* be like.

For many involved in church life, Sundays leave us feeling exhausted and depleted. Some churches, in their advertisements for a new minister, say, "This is a busy church", as if it is a good thing. We have reversed the fourth commandment, making it bad to obey the instruction and good to disobey it. This is a disease of empire; this is the spirit of empire. It wants us to work all the hours God has given and still demands even more. Despite the fact that we live in a liberal democracy, we too are like slaves to the many powers and corporate identities that we live amongst. Our souls are not free.

We are chased by mobile phone calls, emails, texts and tweets. This "fast" approach to life tends to make us controlling, hurried, superficial and impatient—even aggressive and belligerent. In contrast, a "slow" life helps us to feel calm, and give and receive love. It is a way of life where we can be more open and receptive—intuitive, patient and reflective. One cannot help but think of Jesus spending days walking everywhere—having time for people, especially his disciples. High speed and hurried did not exist for him. It is not hard to see how he fitted into the rhythm of life with his Father. At times he worked very hard, but he never rushed. There is a difference.

I found Richard Rohr's work extremely helpful many years ago when I became too busy and over-stressed as a vicar in inner-city Birmingham.[3] Eventually, I had to take time off because I was so ill. In different ways, Rohr suggests it is not so much the sin we commit that keeps us from God, but rather our busyness. When I collapsed in exhaustion, I did not sense closeness to God. It felt like darkness.

I hear so many people complain about the hectic pace of their lives. Our culture teaches us faster is better. In the race to keep ahead, everything suffers—our work, diet and health, our relationships and sex lives. We tend to ignore the things that are most important to us, but not those that are urgent. Sabbath time is a life-saver for us. It prioritises the things that are important rather than urgent, like eating together as a family, celebrating as a community, or simply taking time to smell the flowers, feel the wind and give thanks. We think a fast approach to life will give us all we need, whereas it drains everything from us. Sabbath takes the slow lane.

Somebody who is not in charge of their time (because time is in charge of them) is a slave. Busyness is the culture of empire, not the culture of God. This is today's culture, where many of us are slaves.

The True Self and the False Self

The quest of the spiritual life is to live less on the circumference of life and more from its centre. If we do not make the arduous, inner spiritual journey, the only way to cope with from day to day is to emphasise the outer life. This is why we then spend much of our time reinforcing it. We do not find the alternative—to rest in God—easy.

The problem with living so much of our lives this way is that we end up thinking this externalised self is who we really are. This, though, is only who we *think* we are and who other people *think* we are. It is not who we *really* are. Sadly, we often believe we are our thinking. The externalised life is, at the end of the day, a construction of the mind. It is made up of our roles in life, our reputation, status, and responsibilities. For some, this adds up to a positive self-image, as they are able to spend much of their lives being smart, good-looking, successful and clever. Others do not have this advantage. Their self-image may be quite negative, but it will nonetheless still be centred around what they think of themselves and who they think they are. They may well noisily promote this self-image by constantly telling you how ill they are, how they are always left out and rejected, or speaking proudly about how badly behaved they have been. Thomas Merton called both the negative and the positive self-image the False Self. The life hidden deep within us, and who we really are, Merton called the True Self. There is so much more to us than what we think.

In trying to sort out the wrong in our lives, we have traditionally believed our problem to be a moral problem. We have, therefore, tried to behave differently—doing fewer things that are wrong and doing more things that are right. By the force of our will, we have tried to be good. This appears to be very worthy, but it is a very hard way to live and ultimately does not work. In one of his letters, Paul made this very point:

> I can will what is right, but I cannot do it. For I do not do
> the good I want, but the evil I do not want is what I do.
> (Rom. 7:18–19)

We have to realise that sorting out this mess is not, in the first instance, a moral issue, but a spiritual one. Attempting to do right things will not solve the problem. In fact, it may well make things much worse.

What is important to note about the externalised False Self is it is not necessarily wrong; it is just not the True Self! Roles and responsibilities are crucially important in life. I have always said that if my wife and I did not act in the role of parents, our children would rarely have made it to school. If there were not police officers, paramedics, plumbers and politicians, life would be crazy and chaotic. The False Self becomes a problem only when we think this is who we are—when we over-identify with it. The True Self, the spirit, is who we really are. Living from here changes everything.

We have grown up feeling the False Self is real and robust, but the True Self is terribly fragile and possibly not real at all. Surprisingly, this could not be further from the truth. As well as being who we really are, the True Self is completely indestructible. In fact, it cannot be hurt. The False Self, though, is inherently vulnerable and needy. It needs to be constantly reassured it is okay and doing all right. It is anxious to create a good impression, seeking approval for what it does. When it looks out on the world, the False Self is constantly judging, comparing and competing. It is never at ease or rest. In this defensive attitude, the False Self seeks to control, fix and understand its environment in the hope it will shore up and support its fragile state. At the root of our dilemma is the belief that, without some great achievement or impressive mask, we will not be loved or loveable.

When we are offended, it is the False Self that takes offence. It is not possible to offend the True Self. Jesus was angry at times, but never offended. One way to measure how much we live in the False Self is to see how regularly we feel the hurt of offence. It is a way of living where we are constantly looking "out there" for happiness, fulfilment and approval.

Doing this, we attach ourselves to other people demanding they be the source of our happiness. We do not realise that in Christ we have everything; all we have to do is to experience what we already possess. Living from the False Self keeps us from the Christ who is within. Sadly, we spend most of our lives living from the wrong place. This is why we are unhappy.

The True Self is the life of God within us. It is like a watermark running through us. This is the reality Jesus referred to when he said, "The kingdom of God is within you." This is the place where the union between our life and the life of God is so close that it sometimes becomes hard to see where the difference lies. There is nothing we can do to make this more true or less true. This is the life Paul speaks about when he says, "You have died, and your life is hidden with Christ in God" (Col. 3:3).

This True Self is characterised by abundance and security. It does not have the emotional ups and downs of the False Self because it is not the vulnerable self. As it is not the False Self, it does not need to impress, perform or achieve. It is radically all right. There is nothing that can change that. This, our truest self, cannot be thought; it can only be lived. To use another of Paul's phrases, to live from this place is to be "in Christ". The True Self cannot be achieved or worked for; it can only be discovered. It cannot be taken from you; it is eternally you. It is satisfied and content, able to find joy in any situation. As Paul says,

> I have learned to be content with whatever I have. I know
> what it is to have little, and I know what it is to have plenty.
> In any and all circumstances I have learned the secret of
> being well-fed and of going hungry, of having plenty and
> of being in need. (Phil. 4:11–12).

The False Self cannot achieve or obtain such contentment.

If living in the False Self keeps us from God, the big question is, how do we spend more time living from the True Self where God abides? Effort and self-discipline are not sufficient. We need to become dissatisfied with the False Self. We need to arrive at a point in life where keeping this small False Self happy and afloat no longer appeals to us. We then need to learn how to "starve off" this exterior life and give it less time and attention. Spending time in silence is one part of this. This does several things for us. It is a form of fasting from the world of busyness and achieving. From time to time we give ourselves a break from the madness we live in, so we no longer have to perform to this outer world. It gives us a chance to see through the games our mind plays, which are all about keeping the False Self centre stage.

We need to learn to let go of the False Self. This was central to Jesus' message: "I tell you, unless a grain of wheat falls into the earth and dies, it remains just a single grain; but if it dies, it bears much fruit. Those who love their life lose it, and those who hate their life in this world will keep it for eternal life" (John 12:24–25). These verses have at the beginning of them the phrase "Very truly" (*Verily, verily* in our old Bibles, or *Amen, amen* in the original Greek) to emphasise they are really important. Jesus also said, "If any want to become my followers, let them deny themselves and take up their cross daily and follow me" (Luke 9:23). Central to the whole gospel is Jesus' death and resurrection, not just as a one-off event in history, but to serve as the pattern for the whole of life. Jesus taught us about dying and letting go. Letting go of the False Self is what needs to happen, and this can feel like dying, until we see it helps us to spend more time living from the True Self.

Paul continues with the same theme, "I have been crucified with Christ; and it is no longer I who live, but it is Christ who lives in me" (Gal. 2:19–20). He tells the early church members that, as they grow in God, they are always being given "over to death" which then allows God's life to shine through (2 Cor. 4:11). At baptism, we have the great ritual of casting off the False Self symbolised by passing through the "waters of death" and the rising to new life. We mark each person with a symbol of this great mystery, the cross. The principle of dying and rising is something our busy world cannot and will not understand.

We must remember though, the False Self is not inherently bad or wrong. In fact we cannot live without it. To perform my duties and fulfil my responsibilities, I have to take on the role of a clergyman in the Church of England. The person who comes to repair my washing machine has to take on the role of a service engineer. Those who educate our children must take seriously their role as teachers. All of this only becomes a problem when we start to take these roles so seriously that we begin to act as if this is who we really are. At the end of the day, I am not essentially a clergyman in the Church of England; I am a child of God. This is who I am—my identity. At present I have this role within the church, but it may not always be so.

The Self is also important in the development of the child and young person. As they grow up they have to taste their power and sense their own possibilities. It is very sad to see young people who have not been affirmed, built up and encouraged in their early years, as it can leave them debilitated through their adult years. We therefore spend the first part of life building this tower, but in the second part of life, we need to learn the lesson of coming down from it. In a parable, Jesus told a story about a rich man who had far too much grain to store in his barns, so he decided to build even bigger barns. He thought then he would be able to relax and be happy. God, though, calls him a fool. He had not learnt the lesson of letting go (Luke 12:13–21).

When we start to live from a different place, the True Self, not only do we get to know God; we also get to know ourselves. In fact, I cannot get to know God unless I also get to know myself: they are parallel and linked journeys.

Attachments

Having described what the problem is, we are now going to consider what can be done about it. The surprising thing is the problem of the False Self is not actually the False Self. The problem is our attachment to the False Self.

Our attachments are our ties to anything we think we cannot live without, or be happy without. They can be the ties to our money, house, relationship, title, job or reputation. They are the things we believe can, and must, bring us happiness. The truth is we are enslaved by these attachments because we think if we did not have them, life would not be worth living. We try to re-arrange the world around us so we can maintain and embellish them. We do not realise we do not need any *thing* to be happy. What we need to be happy is to be in touch with our True Self and so also in touch with God. Our attachments become a prison to us. If something goes well for us at work, we feel happy. Then, if it goes badly the next day we feel sad. This is not living in freedom. Our sin results from our attachments. I am jealous and angry because I am attached in a wrong way to people and things. When my attachment to them is threatened, I react and become defensive and aggressive. I try to remove the danger of the perceived threat to my image or interests. I desperately try to maintain my reputation.

The priest and psychotherapist, Anthony de Mello (S.J.), said, "If you look carefully you will see that there is one thing and only one thing that causes unhappiness. The name of that thing is Attachment. What is an attachment? It is an emotional state of clinging caused by the belief that without some particular thing or some person you cannot be happy."[4] The False Self seeks satisfaction in having, owning and clinging, but its enjoyment is short-lived and shallow because it feels what it has is not enough.

Diogenes (c.412–323 BC) was an odd sort of ascetic who lived a rough life out of a small barrel eating leftover food, wearing threadbare clothes and sleeping on the streets. He was known for his wisdom and insight. One day, it is claimed, Alexander the Great came to see him and asked him if there was anything he could do for him. "Yes," he replied, "Please will you stand to one side as you are blocking the sunlight?" Diogenes needed nothing to be content or happy except the sunshine, which is free to everybody.

Ironically, once I have allowed my unhealthy attachments to be broken, then I can move to reattaching myself to the people I love, my job, my role, all creation and even to God. Then I will not be attached in a needy or clinging manner, but in a way which gives others freedom rather than enslaving them to my needs. I can then live with them, without the need to manipulate, control or exploit them, or even without them if needs be, and still be free.

Liminal space

It is impossible to get rid of your attachments yourself; something has to happen *to* you. The saints of old said there are only two ways to change and be transformed—one way was through great love and the other was through great suffering. As most of us find it hard to accept great love, it unfortunately has to be through great suffering. This, it seems, is the only thing that will grab our attention.

Liminal space is the term often applied to the place where our attachments are broken and true transformation takes place. *Limen* is Latin for threshold. Not far from where I used to live is the stately home of Chatsworth. As you walk around the large house you become aware of how thick the walls are. Walking from one room to another, you often go through two doors that are very close together, one on each side of these thick walls. The space between these two doors is a threshold—it is liminal space. Phases of our life can be pictured as being like rooms. We can be fairly happy getting along with the tasks of each day; we call this normality. Then, something terrible happens; somebody dies, we are ill or lose our job, or some other catastrophe. It may simply be that life no longer has purpose or meaning. It might no longer feel safe and secure. In a real sense, we are no longer in control and start to suffer. This is liminal space in life. It is as if we have left one room in life where everything worked. Then, before finding ourselves in a new room, we enter uncharted threshold territory and do not like it.

The Biblical representation of liminal space is the desert. It is a place where we cannot fix things, control things or even understand them. It is the experience of the Children of Israel in the wilderness. When we find ourselves in a difficult and hard place, we want to go back into the "room" where we came from. We want life to return to how things were. The Israelites wanted to return to the slavery of Egypt when they found they could not eat meat on a regular basis—but, of course, we cannot go back.

Jesus was often drawing his disciples into these liminal places where they were not in control and all they could do was to trust and wait. It seems that for almost all of us, it is only this kind of suffering which is able to destabilise the False Self. In these desert phases of life, the False Self system no longer works as it used to. Who cares what we have achieved in life if we have suffered a terrible bereavement? It is no longer significant that we have many degrees and a large house if we have just been diagnosed with cancer. These places of uncertainty and vulnerability are the places we will not enter willingly, but they are the places where great transformation takes place. Liminal space is the place we will do anything to avoid, yet is the place God is always leading us to. The exile of the Old Testament was significant liminal space for the people of God. They did not want to be there and they wanted to get back to Jerusalem (as it had been)—but this was not to be.

An excellent example of this transformation in the Bible is the story of Peter. In the middle of the Gospels, at Caesarea Philippi (Mark 8:27–33), Jesus asks his disciples who they, and other people, thought he was. They came up with various answers, but Peter got it right when he declared, "You are the Messiah (the Christ)." I guess Peter felt like such a good boy. Jesus went on to say that he himself had to suffer and die at the hands of the religious authorities. Peter would not accept this, though, and took Jesus to one side and told him off. Jesus, in turn, rebuked Peter, even calling him Satan. Later in the Gospel, after the Last Supper, Jesus took his disciples out to the Mount of Olives (Mark 14:27–31). He was quite straight with his disciples when he told them they would all soon run away and desert him, but Peter was emphatic—he would never leave Jesus even though all the others might. Here, we can hear the False Self of Peter speaking. He does not let people down. He is not that sort. He is not weak like the others. He is Peter! Yet Jesus quietly stated that by the time the cock crowed Peter will have denied him three times. Peter was then even more emphatic: "Even though I must die with you, I will not deny you" (Mark 14:31). Later that night the cock crowed and Peter realised he had denied Jesus, three times, as predicted. He broke down and wept tears of bitterness. His sense of ego had been truly humiliated; his False Self destabilised.

For me, one of the most beautiful passages in the Bible is when Jesus later reinstates Peter after the resurrection on the shores of Lake Galilee (John 21:15–19). A fish breakfast was eaten around a fire on the lake shore. This must have been an uncomfortable time for Peter. He would have been filled with regret and guilt after he had abandoned Jesus in his hour of need, especially when he had said so boldly it would not happen. When the breakfast had been eaten, Jesus came over to talk to him. My guess is that Peter braced himself, expecting Jesus to ask him why he had turned his back on him and denied him—but Jesus did not ask Peter to account for himself. He simply asked him if he loved him. When Peter answered "Yes", in the best way he could, Jesus simply asked him to become a pastor of others. Nothing was said about his denial and betrayal of Jesus, nothing at all!

At the beginning of this saga, we see Peter as right, self-assured and wilful—telling Jesus what to do. After he has denied ever knowing Jesus, we see him falling uncontrollably into liminal space. He did not like it. He did not want to be there. Only through such a process, though, could his strong attachment to his self-image could be weakened and eroded. Only after that could he be restored. When we read later in the Bible the letters of Peter, it is hard to imagine he was ever the same person.

Regrettably, conversion is a set of necessary humiliations of the False Self. When life leads us into the valley of the shadow of death, there is then the possibility of transformation. Nothing lives until it dies. This is the great mystery of the cross and the death and resurrection of Jesus.

None of us responds well to suffering and humiliation. They are inevitable, though, and dare I say even necessary. Sadly, the church has not been effective in teaching this great truth of the gospel, instead preferring the worldly lesson of "onwards and upwards". That may be the motto of empire, but it is not the motto of the kingdom of God—death and resurrection is.

"Flesh" in Paul's writings

Paul, of course, does not use Merton's language of the False Self. There is a word he does use, but it is not easy to translate. It is the Greek word *sarx*. It is often translated into English as "flesh", but would be more helpfully translated as the False Self.[5] The problem with using flesh as the translation is it has led us to believe Paul was against the body, sex and anything physical—but this word "flesh" does not mean the body. Yet this negative way of regarding Paul's writings has persisted over generations. Paul believed in the creation; in all that was natural and physical. He rejected the Greek idea that separated the spiritual from the physical (he used a different word for the body, *soma*, used in phrases such as "the body of Christ" and the church's "one body with many members").

It is helpful then, to replace the word "flesh" in St Paul's writings with the term "False Self", and replace "our spirit" with the phrase "True Self", as follows in selected verses from Romans 8:

> [1] There is therefore now no condemnation for those who are in Christ Jesus.
>
> [5] For those who live according to the *False Self* set their minds on the things of the *False Self*, but those who live according to the Spirit set their minds on the things of the Spirit.
>
> [6] To set the mind on the *False Self* is death, but to set the mind on the Spirit is life and peace. [7] For this reason the mind that is set on the *False Self* is hostile to God; it does not submit to God's law—indeed it cannot, [8] and those who are in the *False Self* cannot please God.
>
> [12] So then, brothers and sisters, we are debtors, not to the *False Self*, to live according to the *False Self*—[13] for if you live according to the *False Self*, you will die; but if by the Spirit you put to death the deeds of the body, you will live.
>
> [14] For all who are led by the Spirit of God are children of God. [15] For you did not receive a spirit of slavery to fall back into fear, but you have received a spirit of adoption. When we cry, "Abba! Father!" [16] it is that very Spirit bearing witness with our *True Self* that we are children of God, [17] and if children, then heirs, heirs of God and joint heirs with Christ—if, in fact, we suffer with him so that we may also be glorified with him.

Put this way, it is clear that Paul sees the False Self has no future, as it does not lead to life. He even uses the language of slavery to describe what it is to fall back into living the fearful way of the False Self (8:15).

Living in the present moment

The mind is not at ease living in the here and now. To keep us living in the False Self, the old patterns of the mind constantly pull us out of the present moment to some point in the past or the future, or to a different place geographically. To defend and promote the False Self, the mind is constantly travelling out of the present moment. If we sit and observe our thoughts, we discover that they almost always take us to a different point in time. Some people tend to be more "backward reflectors". They spend more time in the past than others of us. As they look back, they could be justifying something they did, which others disagreed with, in a vain attempt to buttress the False Self. They could also be looking back nostalgically, to when life seemed better and sweeter. Some people look backwards and criticise themselves. Thinking like this takes a person out of the present moment. Other people tend to spend more time looking forward. They could be anticipating a future threat to their reputation or self-image, thinking about how they might "save face" when the moment arises. Some people look ahead with the hope the future will be a better and brighter day than today. They are living in the future and missing out on the present.

Whether people are looking backwards or forwards, they are not present in the here and now. Looking at someone in one of these states we might conclude, "The lights are on but there is no one in." We cannot live in the past or the future; we can only live in the present. We cannot love in the past or the future; you can only love now, today. The mind does not know what to do with the present, though. This is one of the first problems people encounter when they introduce some silence into their lives: their minds take them out of the present moment. I am most alive though, when I am fully present in this moment of time. This is when I sense and feel my True Self. This point in time does not have to be defended or protected. All we can do is to submit to the beauty of the moment, whether we are in the middle of a crisis or a celebration; a birth or a death.

I once knew of a vicar who was leading the important eucharistic prayer during the communion service. Part way through it he lost his place as he had let his mind wander on to other things, away from the moment. He quietly turned to his curate, who was kneeling nearby, and asked where he was up to. The curate replied, "I have no idea!" Neither of them was present in the moment. Following the advice from one of my former bishops, I now quietly ask myself before I start the communion prayer, if I am present. I touch the communion table firmly with my hand to help me do this. The present moment can only be lived in and sensed, it cannot experienced by thinking. Somehow, touching something or somebody can help us be there. This is why we eat bread and drink wine at communion; to help us be present to the presence of Christ. This is why we touch the people we love. When I am comparing myself with other people and competing with them, though, I am not in love and I am not here. When I am in the present moment I am living as my True Self and cannot help but love.

In contemplative prayer, we are seeking to live and breathe the present, as this is where God is. We cannot know God in the past or the future, only in the present. I may know *about* God in the past, but this is an activity of the mind and is different to knowing in the present moment, which is to love. The psychiatrist and contemplative theologian, Gerald May, believes contemplation happens to everyone when they are open, undefended, and immediately present.[6]

Using silence

One of the great diseases of our time is we are too goal-orientated. We feel there is somewhere we need to get to. The truth is that we are already here, we just have not realised it yet. Everything we need is here in this moment and is not conditional on us doing anything. I often try and remind myself of the truth that there is nothing I can do to make God like me more or love me more, and there is nothing I can do to make God like me less or love me less. If I do have a task, it is to become aware I am already loved.

Too many Christians are wracked by guilt and feel they must be doing more or praying harder to reach God. This is true even among those who say they believe in justification by faith. It has been said that our feelings of guilt and shame result from the False Self kicking back in an attempt to make us take on responsibility for our own healing and wholeness, as if we can save ourselves. Having this as a starting point leads nowhere.

By its nature, the spirit is slow. Learning to use silence in life and in prayer cannot be rushed. We must slow down to connect with ourselves, with each other, with creation and with God.

The Quaker, Parker Palmer, asks how we are to slow down and pay attention, as attention is not a skill many of us possess. He paints a delicate picture:

> In our culture, we tend to gather information in ways that do not work very well when the source is the human soul: the soul is not responsive to subpoenas or cross-examinations . . . The soul is like a wild animal—tough, resilient, savvy, self-sufficient, and yet exceedingly shy. If we want to see a wild animal, the last thing we should do is to go crashing through the woods, shouting for the creature to come out. But if we are willing to walk quietly into the woods and sit silently for an hour or two at the base of a tree, the creature we are waiting for may well emerge, and out of the corner of our eye we will catch a glimpse of the precious wildness we seek.[7]

Prayer is not about perfecting a technique; it is learning to be present to God who is always present to us. It is about learning to live with and alongside the inner witness of the Holy Spirit. We do not have to generate it, or cause it to happen, but we do have to be watchful. As Jesus said, we must watch and pray. If lovers only ever talked incessantly, without slipping into silence where they just touch and join, then it would not be much of a relationship. Paul says our prayer leads to the peace of God, which "surpasses all understanding" (Phil. 4:7). It goes beyond knowing with our heads to the joining of our lives. When we are joined with God's life, then we are truly alive and fully human.

We need to learn to live God's way as expressed at Sinai, demanded by the prophets and demonstrated by Jesus in his kingdom way of living. In this we find Sabbath rest and silence.

Questions for discussion

1. On a score of 1 to 10, how busy is your life? Do you think this should change? If so, how will you do it?
2. What moments of liminal space have there been in your life? When you came through these, did you feel better or bitter? What lessons did these times teach you?
3. Spend some time in silence. Spend ten minutes longer than you are used to. Share with others what you felt about it. What were the distractions? What were the gifts?
4. In what way does the power of the False Self in your life affect the way you behave and the choices you make? Does the idea that the True Self is indestructible seem believable to you? Share times when you know you have been living from the True Self and what the fruit was.
5. What do you think Jesus meant when he said that anyone who wants to be his disciple must deny themselves and take up their cross daily and follow him?

Prayer

O voice of God,
    who often comes
    not through great and mighty winds,
    not in terror inducing earthquakes,
    nor by rushing consuming fires,

but simply
in still, small speaking
after all else
has died down;
lead us
into the sound of sheer silence
until we have learnt lessons
that can only be received
in deserted
and wild spaces of emptiness.
Amen.

Notes

1. Thomas Merton, *New Seeds of Contemplation* (New Directions, 1972).

2. Abraham Joshua Heschel, *The Sabbath: Its Meaning for the Modern Man* (Farrar, Straus and Giroux, 2005), p. 16.

3. Richard Rohr, *Everything Belongs: The Gift of Contemplative Prayer* (Crossroad, 2003). Richard Rohr, *True Self False Self* (Compact Disc Edition) (St Anthony Messenger Press, 2003).

4. Anthony de Mello, *The Way to Love* (Image, 1995), p. 28.

5. Thomas Keating, *Foundations for Centering Prayer and the Christian Contemplative Life: Open Mind, Open Heart / Invitation to Love / Mystery of Christ* (Continuum, 2006), p. 165.

6. Robert J. Wicks (Ed.), *Handbook of Spirituality for Ministers, Volume 2: Perspectives for the 21st Century* (Paulist Press, 2000), p. 420.

7. Parker J. Palmer, *Let Your Life Speak: Listening for the Voice of Vocation* (Jossey-Bass, 2000), p. 7.

CHAPTER 7

After Exile

History is a succession of empires and kingdoms. This was true in the Old Testament just as it has been true throughout our European history. Israel's downfall was its aspiration to be "like the other nations". As a community, they thought nationhood would set them up as a secure and significant people. These other nations appeared to them to be more important than they were and seemed to be prospering—but this way is the predictable pattern of empire which ultimately robs people of their humanity.

This same aspiration to be like others is true in our personal lives. God offers us an alternative way to live that trusts something deeper within us, but it seems all too unbelievably simple. We do not believe or trust it. Just as Israel looked to the nations around it, we too look to others who appear, in our eyes, to be more successful and more significant than we are, and also have more than we have. We want to be like them, have what they have and do what they do. In short, we break the commandments and covet what others have.

The fall of Jerusalem changed all of this for God's people. It cannot be over-emphasised how severe the trauma of exile was. The year 587 BC, which brought this disaster, has been indelibly marked in the minds of Jews ever since. In fact, much of the Old Testament was written in response to this crisis, in order to try and make sense of their nightmare. What was thought impossible had happened. The promises of God appeared to have come to nothing. Devastation was not too strong a word. Even though it was more comfortable, exile in Babylon was a worse experience than slavery in Egypt. In Babylon they were so aware of what they had lost, or what they *thought* they had lost.

In their grief they sat and endlessly mulled over this loss. It is no wonder a third of the Psalms are songs of lament: they could not find consolation in exile. Life was too painful and chaotic. Only God could make something good come out of it. In time, they realised this terrible state of affairs had arisen because they had ignored Sinai. It was as if they were married to God, but behaved as if they were not. The powerful drive of the collective ego led them to look elsewhere for what only God could give them—a sense of belonging, identity and purpose.

In exile they had to face such questions as: Have we got a future? Is there any hope? Will God do anything new for us or is it all over? It did not look as if they had a future. However, in Biblical faith, God sometimes acts beyond our wildest expectations. Now Israel had to see if deep down it believed this was still true.

Coming out of exile

Exile in Babylon lasted 49 years. Not all of those who had been transported into captivity returned. Some rather liked the way of life in what had now become the Persian Empire, as Babylon had itself been defeated. They assimilated and settled for the easy option, choosing not to return to the ruins of Jerusalem. This phase in the life of God's people marks the start of what is often referred to as the post-exilic period. It is a period Christians have not always paid a lot of attention to. More recently though, scholars have been researching it once again, and this is helping us to realise how important this time was in the development of Israel, and how it might be important for us in understanding our situation today.

While exile ended technically and geographically after 49 years, spiritually and theologically the Jews remained in exile for centuries. The gospels lead us to believe they were only understood as properly emerging from it with the coming of Jesus. Even though a new temple was built after 520 BC, it was always considered to be a shadow of the glory of the first one. The people were never really in charge of their own affairs again as a succession of empires dominated them, taxed them and compromised their standing with God. You might think this was a depressing and totally barren period in their history, but this is not true. It was while in these apparently barren years, this liminal space between the nation they had once been and the one they still hoped to be, that the people were able to reconnect with God on different terms; not on the terms of empire. It was while on the brink of what seemed to be never-ending despair that hope was found, when the ancient texts, which had been handed down over the generations, became ever more important to God's people. They remembered their story and their origins. In this period, the role of the prophets once again became significant.

The prophets

An amazingly large part of the Bible is devoted to the prophets—but who were they? As I have already stated they were rarely establishment people. As they did not have any vested interests, they did not compromise their message: they were free to speak. Most of them were poets of a sort. Many of their texts in our Bibles have been laid out in a manner which reflects this.

Poetry is a special way of speaking. It is not a straight, flat prose that speaks in an over-explained manner. Poets are not trying to pass advice on to people. They speak in ways which are open and permeable; ways that help people see things differently. They do not try to persuade people; instead they surprise, stimulate and provoke. Prophetic poetry speaks of what cannot be seen and what no one dares name, often using ambiguous language. It draws the listener in to do their own work, so they find their way to a new place through the poetry. To do this, the Jewish prophets sang songs, recited poems and sometimes acted out their message in strange ways, even by doing odd things such as walking naked in public (Isa. 20:1–3), laying on one side for over a year (Ezek. 4:1–4) or burning their hair (Ezek. 5:1–2). Some prophets were the equivalent of our street poets today: people who are more on the edge of the community than at its centre. The prophetic books that bear their names are more a collection of sayings and poems than anything else.

The prophets seemed to specialise in upsetting the status quo, making it their business to afflict the comfortable, while comforting the afflicted. This sort of poetry is not the language of empire; that prefers direct, linear language with watertight certainties. Poets speak about matters others would rather ignore and talk publicly of things many powerful people would rather they did not mention.

In the months leading up to the fall of the Berlin Wall, the people of Leipzig crowded into churches, the only safe places to congregate in the city. They did this to recite poetry, play music and pray, along with reading stories. What needed to be said could only be expressed in these forms of speech. One evening, 120,000 people emerged from these churches with candles onto the streets. They encircled the city with light. They were scared the military would turn their guns on them. However, it was the communist regime which eventually collapsed, and it toppled without violence.

In Harare, the capital city of Zimbabwe, a venue called the Book Café provides an environment where both performers and audience can debate, challenge and confront the injustices in their country. It is a meeting place for poets of protest where a leading Zimbabwean poet, Samm Farai Monro, says that you have to have guts to say what you want and spit it out in a poem. The café has been attacked, persecuted and shut down repeatedly over the years.

Biblical prophets share much in common with these poets. They were like dissident intellectuals who refused to do things and say things the way the establishment wanted them done and said. They condemned the crimes of state and the deplorable conduct of those who held power. These Jewish prophets had an amazing capacity for criticism of their own nation and establishment. This is not a characteristic of empires. The people of empire employ good PR to make evil look righteous and gloss over inconvenient truths. The prophets had the guts to tell their own people, "We have got it wrong."

Einstein said you cannot solve a problem with the same consciousness which caused it. Or, to put it more simply, do not try to put something right with the same mentality that made it happen in the first place. The imperial way is to do the same old thing, over and over again, with the hope it will work out differently the next time around. Its way is to win, conquer and defeat, and then maintain control, market share and/or cultural dominance. This does not bring peace and prosperity for all. There are always winners and losers. Prophets see another way; they recognise another consciousness and see alternative possibilities. They are courageous carriers of hope, who hold on to the belief that God has still got something to do.

Texts of hope

Martin Luther King Jr was a prophet/poet who carried hope and imagination. In his most popular "I have a dream" speech, as well as in many others, he was able to bring to voice what others could not imagine, but he could see in his mind's eye. While rooting his speech in the American Constitution, he was able to envision a time when enemies would one day share a meal together; injustice and oppression would be transformed into freedom and justice; people would not be judged by the colour of their skin, only by their character. This was the hope he saw and the dream he dreamed.

Prophets like Martin Luther King are those whose visions have the ability to change the course of history. Their mixture of imagination and risk leads people to newness when all they have known is loss, despair and desolation. It is, of course, those people who dwell in the land of darkness who can best see the light of God's future.

We will now look at texts from three of the prophets that illustrate this: Ezekiel, Isaiah and Zechariah. I will then explain how a new type of message emerges in the book of Daniel.

Ezekiel

If there is a bizarre book in the Old Testament, it is the book of Ezekiel. This prophet was a man of great faith and imagination. His visions are grand and symbolic. They communicate his insights about God's people in exile; what God might do about the restoration of Israel. He knew there needed to be a new heart in Israel and nothing was going to happen without God's agent, the Spirit, acting. He was a priest as well as a prophet who cared for the people while in exile. He had a special interest in the people's worship.

When the ruling elite were forcibly taken to Babylon, they were not kept in prisons or detention centres. They were free to get on with life as they wished. Some did quite well out of this new life and became wealthy. They were free to meet together, elect leaders and worship—but it was hard to worship while in exile. They could never get the destruction of Jerusalem, their holy city with its wonderful temple, out of their heads. They refused to "sing the Lord's song in a foreign land" (Ps. 137:4). For most of them, they were not where they wanted to be, they wanted to go home.

Eventually, when they were encouraged to go back to Jerusalem, many had lost heart. The old dream of living with God had died and was buried under their despair. Then, one day, the Spirit of God took hold of the prophet Ezekiel, taking him in his mind's eye to a valley filled with dry bones. Here is how the vision unfolded:

> He led me all round them; there were very many lying in the valley, and they were very dry. He said to me, "Mortal, can these bones live?" I answered, "O Lord God, you know." Then he said to me, "Prophesy to these bones, and say to them: O dry bones, hear the word of the Lord. Thus says the Lord God to these bones: I will cause breath to enter you, and you shall live. I will lay sinews on you, and will cause flesh to come upon you, and cover you with skin, and put breath in you, and you shall live; and you shall know that I am the Lord."
>
> So I prophesied as I had been commanded; and as I prophesied, suddenly there was a noise, a rattling, and the

bones came together, bone to its bone. I looked, and there were sinews on them, and flesh had come upon them, and skin had covered them; but there was no breath in them. Then he said to me, "Prophesy to the breath, prophesy, mortal, and say to the breath: Thus says the Lord God: Come from the four winds, O breath, and breathe upon these slain, that they may live." I prophesied as he commanded me, and the breath came into them, and they lived, and stood on their feet, a vast multitude.

Then he said to me, "Mortal, these bones are the whole house of Israel. They say, 'Our bones are dried up, and our hope is lost; we are cut off completely.' Therefore prophesy, and say to them, Thus says the Lord God: I am going to open your graves, and bring you up from your graves, O my people; and I will bring you back to the land of Israel. And you shall know that I am the Lord, when I open your graves, and bring you up from your graves, O my people. I will put my spirit within you, and you shall live, and I will place you on your own soil; then you shall know that I, the Lord, have spoken and will act, says the Lord." (Ezek. 37:1–14)

All had seemed lost. Even the exiles' weakest hopes had been dashed. They saw themselves as being like dead people. Jerusalem repeated with one voice, "The Lord has forsaken me, the Lord has forgotten me" (Isa. 49:14). This is a "Prodigal Son" type story, but situated in the Old Testament. Beneath the despair and feelings of death was a crushed and hopeless people. No wonder many decided to throw their lot in with the empire: it was easier to abandon their faith than seek to rekindle it.

In this vision of the valley of dry bones, Ezekiel was asked whether the bones could live. He could not say, but he was sure God knew. When all seemed lost, God still had the potential to act. It was only when grief was at its deepest that newness could emerge. For resurrection to happen there first has to be death.

Today, we too live in a type of exile. We have lost much from our faith. Christianity does not seem as robust in the West as it used to be.

Churches are weaker. Our faith is not so much despised in the public arena as simply ignored. Many of our children and grandchildren have not continued with our habits and traditions of the faith. We too try to get back to our "promised land" when we thought we had it right with stronger church attendance and faith central to our families and nation. We have to learn, like the exiles, that when we are dying and dead we can do nothing—but God can: "Then you shall know that I, the Lord, have spoken and will act" (Ezek. 37:14). It is only God who can bring something truly new. It was the prophets who usually got a sense of this before anyone else. They knew God chooses to act unilaterally to bring restoration. Exile is not the last word and neither is death.

Isaiah

The writings in Isaiah relate to a period which starts a hundred years before the exile right through to the time when the people were back in Jerusalem. The later readings we find in Isaiah 56–66 reassured the captives after their return that, despite how bad things looked, God would do something. The prophets spoke out in support of the many priests who felt side-lined in Babylon because they had remembered the principle of Jubilee, when most people had simply forgotten Sinai. They caught hold of the old idea again that allowed excluded people the opportunity to participate again in the life of the community.

> The spirit of the Lord God is upon me,
>   because the Lord has anointed me;
> he has sent me to bring good news to the oppressed,
>   to bind up the broken-hearted,
> to proclaim liberty to the captives,
>   and release to the prisoners;
> to proclaim the year of the Lord's favour,
>   and the day of vengeance of our God;
>   to comfort all who mourn. (Isa. 61:1–2)

The words "the year of the Lord's favour" are a link to the Jubilee we encountered earlier (Lev. 25) where the poor are allowed to share in the wealth of the community. We also have here the common theme of liberation of captives. In ancient times, many poor people were imprisoned by their inability to pay their debts. In this passage, we have a clear declaration in the midst of empire, even while now back in Jerusalem, that God stands for something entirely different. Through Jubilee, God acts and breaks entrenched patterns of injustice.

The sketch which is painted in these verses comes from a fresh imagination. It gives a sense of what the fruit of salvation for Jerusalem will be—and it is not the oppression of empire. Hearing of such newness helps the people resist the pull of the "wrong way", which always seeks to entice them back into slavery. Significantly, Jesus refers to this passage at the start his ministry (Luke 4:18–19). It is a clear marker that he will follow in the traditions of the prophets and that his kingdom is rooted in the good news of Jubilee.

Zechariah

The book of Zechariah can be divided into two parts. Chapters 1–8 are a series of prophecies and visions which look forward towards a time when worship and community will be re-established under God's oversight. Chapters 9–14 are a collection of messages about the coming of a specially anointed person, a Messiah, and what he will do. In the passage below, we read words that are familiar to churchgoers on Palm Sunday:

> Rejoice greatly, O daughter Zion!
>> Shout aloud, O daughter Jerusalem!
> Lo, your king comes to you;
>> triumphant and victorious is he,
> humble and riding on a donkey,
>> on a colt, the foal of a donkey.

> He will cut off the chariot from Ephraim
>   and the warhorse from Jerusalem;
> and the battle-bow shall be cut off,
>   and he shall command peace to the nations;
> his dominion shall be from sea to sea,
> and from the River to the ends of the earth.
> As for you also, because of the blood of my covenant
>   with you,
>   I will set your prisoners free from the waterless pit.
> Return to your stronghold, O prisoners of hope;
>   today I declare that I will restore to
>   you double. (Zech. 9:9–12)

This message also stands in the great justice tradition of Israel with its roots in Moses and the Ten Commandments. It speaks of the special one coming: not as a victorious, pompous and arrogant emperor, but in humility; not on the preferred imperial transport of a war-horse, but on a donkey (9:9). This Messiah will remove weapons of war from God's people, weapons they were never supposed to have had in the first place (9:10). Hope is re-established (9:11–12).

It is significant that both Matthew and John apply this passage to Jesus in their gospels as he enters Jerusalem before his trial and crucifixion. Jesus enters town in a manner described by Zechariah (Matt. 21:5, John 12:15–16). He refuses to enter the city as Roman leaders did. Instead he stages this street drama, a prophetic act, to make a point demonstrating a radically different way of being a king. In this text, the hope of a Messiah is no longer an aspiration to be "like the other nations".

Daniel

Despite returning back to Jerusalem, the Jews still lived under one empire or another most of the time. In the second century before Christ, they found themselves under what remained of Alexander the Great's Hellenistic (Greek) empire. While Babylon and Persia were basically militaristic empires, the Jews now suffered cultural rather than military domination.

They were an odd group of people who would not fit into any sort of Hellenistic regime as they were uncompromisingly loyal to one God. They refused to worship the emperor or participate in his cults. Instead, they followed the way of the law and practised the rituals of their faith in order to preserve their identity.

The book of Daniel poses this question: how much imperial life can you engage in without ceasing to be Jews? This question was not new; it had been raised many times before. To what extent can you accommodate the ways of empire, compromise your faith and still be a Jew? It is a question we must ask ourselves too. We have to ask how far we can go as followers of Jesus Christ in involving ourselves in the business of the empires we live among without compromising our identity. Western cultures, corporations and retail empires are not always hospitable to the way of Jesus. How are we supposed to live in a place where Sabbath rest is ignored and advertising is about enticing people to have what others have got (the temptation of covetousness)?

We find it hard to agree as Christians how we should live in such a context because it is almost impossible to live without dealing with empires in one way or another. This was true in Biblical times too. Different people and different communities did not always agree about how involved they could become with the powers-that-be. Esther took a very hard line and was quite uncompromising. Ezra took a softer line. He said the people must obey the laws of God *and* of the Emperor. God's people have always debated these issues, from Old Testament times right through until today. In the Old Testament we have a selection of different stories which deal with the matter and propose different solutions.

In the second century BC, the Jews found themselves again struggling to preserve their loyalty to God. Again, the temptation was to give in to the easier option—the way of empire. The book of Daniel was written to help the Jews with this struggle. Most of us grew up with the story of the fiery furnace (Dan. 3). This is a classic story about three Hebrew men named originally named as Hannaniah, Mishael and Azariah. These were three good Jewish men with typical Jewish names, but their names were changed. They were given names from the empire, the three we know well: Shadrach, Meshach and Abednego (Dan. 1:7). Here is an attempt to sideline their Jewishness. Daniel also had his name changed, to Belteshazzar. Cultures have done this regularly. I am reminded of Elton John's song "Candle in the Wind". The ballad tells how the film industry made the star take on a new name, Marilyn Monroe: "They set you on the treadmill, and they made you change your name."

Daniel, Hannaniah, Mishael and Azariah (now renamed as Belteshazzar, Shadrach, Meshach and Abednego) were supposed to pretend they were not Jews, did not read the Ten Commandments or eat kosher food (Dan. 1:8). They were supposed to give in to the treadmill of empire.

To the question, "How do you keep your faith identity while in empire?" Daniel would answer, "You keep it by being a hoper." I have to be honest, I am not optimistic about the future of the church in Britain, but I am hopeful. Things may not turn out as we want them to be with ever-growing churches full of confidence and vitality. God will come with his newness when we have stopped trying to regain control, success and dominance. He may not act during our lifetime, but when he does, it will almost certainly not be what we are expecting or even wanting.

Back in the story of Daniel, things became so desperate that the Jews no longer believed God would work from *within* history. Things were so wretched that no action from within time and space could be imagined which would be able restore Israel. Life had become so unbearable—faith impossible to practise. However, they stubbornly refused to give into the dominance of the empire. The second half of the book of Daniel deals with this new development in the struggle to maintain faith, often via weird and peculiar images and visions. Now hope is pushed *outside* of history. God's people believed nothing from within history was able to save them, but significant change would only come from outside of space and time, through great cosmic upheaval. When it comes, though, it will change everything. God will come and end the whole world system as we know it, bringing in a new regime called the kingdom of God.

Daniel 7:9–14 is poetry rather than narrative. The prophet "saw" in his mind's eye that a new government was formed and one called the "Ancient of Days" was seated on the throne. To us, this is not easy language. For the people of God in the second century BC, however, it was hopeful language. It was a conviction that God will, one day, defeat the empires of the world; that all things will be well. This faith which moved from within history to beyond history is called "apocalyptic faith". It is out of this world. It cannot be accurately described from within this world, only alluded to, hence the highly symbolic language.

Daniel 7:13 is a very significant verse: "I saw one like a human being (Son of Man) coming with the clouds of heaven." The vision affirms the Son of Man (from beyond history) will be God's agent. This term "Son of Man" is the only name Jesus applied to himself consistently throughout his ministry. (He did not call himself Son of God or Lord: other people did.) In the middle of the cosmic upheaval it will not be a superman or a violent emperor who will come to save his people, but a human who would ultimately hang on a cross before being raised to life three days later.

In the book of Daniel we read about men who participated at the heart of society in the empire's version of the civil service. They believed you could deal with the empire—but they were also totally uncompromising when it came to trusting the one God and praying to him. The book of the prophet Daniel gives hope to a people who thought everything was stacked against them. It was during this time that their hope became a massive hope which reached beyond their provincial problems, and beyond the world.

Both the Exodus and Exile stories, with their lessons of loss and new beginnings, are crucial to understanding the Old Testament story. As we shall see with Jesus, the spiritual journey is all about losing and finding, dying and rising. Through their Exodus, the Children of Israel embarked on a journey to become a people whose values and worship would be quite different to what they had known in Egypt, although it was short-lived. Exile was a devastating story of loss for Israel, but through it came the scriptures and the realisation of a promised Messiah.

Today's crises might not seem to us as acute as the destruction of Jerusalem at the hands of the Babylonians, but many believe them as serious. There is a sense that we have lost something in society, in the church and in our own lives. To deal with this loss, we often try to "work the problem" and get control over our destiny again. We do not take time to admit and feel our grief, while waiting for God to act with newness and resurrection.

In our present predicament we can do one of several things:

- Fight to try and preserve what we have;
- Get angry and look for someone to blame;
- Give in to despair and become fatalistic; or
- Look to God in our loss, admit to the pain of our situation and see if we can sense some hope, not baseless optimism, in our darkness.

We must dig deep in our faith and in our texts if we are to find this hope. This is not a time for easy pragmatic solutions; that is the way of empire. As the (re-arranged) saying goes, "Don't just do something, sit there!"

The Old Testament teaches us failure, shame, disintegration and despair are not the end. When we have fallen way beyond our comfort, security and safety zones, we find God—a God who still acts. It is one of the most important lessons we learn in the first part of our Bible, the Old Testament. This, then, sets the scene as we now move on to the New Testament.

Questions for discussion

1. What is the most devastating experience you have ever suffered? At what point did you start to sense hope again?
2. Who are the dissident intellectual poets of our day? Can you share any examples of their poetry? What is it about Martin Luther King's "I have a dream" speech that catches people's imagination?
3. Read Jesus' parable of the Prodigal Son (Luke 15:11–32). In what ways is this also the story of God's people in the Old Testament?
4. Do we need fresh "prophetic imagination" today as we explain decline in the church, the economy and Western culture? Are we prone as the church to try to fix these problems rather than

admitting to our grief, feeling our loss and waiting for God's newness?

5. Why do you think many of our children and grandchildren have not participated in the faith and the life of the church as we have?

Prayer

We mistakenly believe
 that we freely make choices
 in the way that we live our lives.
Yet, if we are honest,
 we know we live in a world of influences, pressures
 and seductions
 which steer and guide
 the way we live our lives,
 determine our purchases,
 use our time
 and what we think is important.
Help us to become people of hope
 who expect
 and look
 for you to work again
in new, exciting, frightening and threatening ways,
so that we might not lose our identity
 or submit to despair,
 as the empires would have us do.
Amen.

CHAPTER 8

Jesus and Empire

As we move into the New Testament, we begin with the Gospels. There is continuity between the two parts of the Bible. The story of the New Testament is, in essence, the same story of the Old Testament, but Jesus brings everything into a clearer focus.

The Gospels begin with an awareness of empire. The Jews of Jesus' day were painfully aware they were living under foreign, imperial rule. All that was different to their ancestors' situation in the Old Testament was that a different "nation" lorded it over them. This time, the oppressing empire was the Roman Empire. It seemed as if little had changed since the exile. Even the main question remained much the same: "If Israel was truly God's people, how come the pagans were ruling over them?" Many things appeared the same because their situation spiritually and theologically was no different—they had not yet properly left exile.

The birth of Jesus

The Gospels of Matthew and Luke start with a baby king (or at least one anointed to be a king). It looked as if Jesus was set to usurp the place of the imperial ruler, Caesar.

The birth narratives are full of names and titles that sound, to some people today, like religious jargon. The baby Joseph named "Jesus" was also given other titles: Son of God, Prince of Peace, Saviour of the World and Lord. We have grown up with these names and, on the whole, have accepted them without much question. What they stood for is crucial, though, if we are to have a true understanding of what was happening at the first Christmas. The politically important character in the story is the Roman Emperor. The text says, "In those days Caesar Augustus issued a decree that a census should be taken" (Luke 2:1). Why did the writer think these details were important enough to be included?

Thirty or forty years before the birth of Jesus, this Caesar Augustus had been regarded as the one who saved the Roman nation from civil war and collapse. As a result, he was showered with the titles Son of God, bringer of Peace, Saviour of the World and Lord for what he had done. In the eyes of the Empire and popular culture he had become a divine figure who had saved the people.

The Biblical story, though, refuses to accept this version of events. Instead, it defiantly declares that this child, lying in the manger, is Son of God, Prince of Peace, Saviour of the World and Lord; not the Emperor on his throne in Rome. Of course, to apply any of these titles to the new born baby Jesus would be regarded as mockery or sedition.

Out in the hill country beyond Bethlehem, the angels declared to the shepherds, "and on earth *peace* to people of goodwill" (Luke 2:14). Peace has always been an important part of the church's Christmas message, but what were the contemporary issues regarding peace at that first Christmas? The Roman Empire was promoted as the bringer of peace. Caesar Augustus had imposed a peace of sorts, through military intervention, on an empire that was hell-bent on destroying itself. Thus, the "whole world" had been brought under the peace of the Roman Empire, often referred to in Latin as *Pax Romana*.

When Mary declared, "My spirit rejoices in *God my Saviour*" (Luke 1:47) after meeting her cousin Elizabeth to share the news she was to have such a special child, and when the angels announced to the shepherds, "To you is born this day in the city of David a *Saviour*, who is the Messiah, the *Lord*" (Luke 2:11), they were not using quaint titles to make the event sound holy and special. To use such titles would have been regarded, at the very least, as subversive: these were only meant for the Emperor. As a result, from the moment of Jesus' conception, we can see that conflict with the Empire would be inevitable. When Luke declared in his Gospel that Jesus was the *Saviour*, he was not using benign religious language; these were loaded words, heavy with meaning. It would have been quite clear to first-century people living in Palestine/Israel it meant the Emperor was not the Saviour, Jesus was.

Mark began his Gospel with a bold statement: "The beginning of the good news of Jesus Christ, the *Son of God*" (Mark 1:1). "Son of God" was a title reserved for one person only—Caesar Augustus. If any loyal Roman citizen was asked, "Who is the Son of God?" they would have looked back at you rather quizzically and replied, "Well, Caesar, of course." Later on in John's Gospel, many Samaritans from a local town believed the testimony of a woman Jesus had been talking with. They said, "We know that this [man] is truly the *Saviour of the world*" (John 4:42). They then knew, and were probably highly relieved, it was not Caesar.

Jesus was the direct opposite of all Caesar Augustus stood for. The empire of Jesus, the kingdom of God, was to bring peace and well-being, not by military domination and political control, but through love, forgiveness and justice. This is quite a different way. This is the age-old way of God.

Wilderness temptations

At the beginning of his ministry, Jesus was baptised. The Spirit came down on him like a dove and a voice said, "You are my Son, the Beloved; with you I am well pleased" (Luke 3:22). Right at the beginning of his mission, his identity was confirmed. Jesus *knew* who he was. He did not have to gain approval from those around him or seek it from the authorities. Kings, pharaohs and emperors have to rely on the might of their kingdoms and empires for their identity. Jesus' identity came from a different place. He was a different sort of king. All he needed was affirmation from his Father.

Immediately following his baptism, confident about who he was, Jesus was led into the wilderness. It was in the desert the Children of Israel had to learn to live in the new economy that God had given them at Sinai, while resisting the temptation and seduction of empire. Jesus now had to follow his journey into liminal space and face the temptations of empire. As his forty days symbolised their forty years, it is no surprise Jesus reaffirmed the importance of the commandments of Mount Sinai.

In the first of the three temptations Matthew's Gospel tells us:

> The tempter came and said to him, "If you are the Son of God, command these stones to become loaves of bread." But he answered, "It is written, 'One does not live by bread alone, but by every word that comes from the mouth of God.'" (Matt. 4:3–4)

This is how Jesus reaffirmed the Ten Commandments. The commandments are recorded in Exodus 20. They are then repeated again in the book of Deuteronomy (5:1–21). This book was the Israelites' attempt to interpret the commandments for their community. The reply Jesus gave the tempter was a direct quotation from this (8:3). The phrase "words that come from the mouth of God" refers to what God revealed at Sinai. Jesus resisted temptation by quoting from the texts which expounded the commandments.

When Jesus was tempted a second time (Matt. 4:5–7) he responded with another quotation from this same part of Deuteronomy, "Again it is written, 'Do not put the Lord your God to the test'" (Deut. 6:16).

Then, with the final temptation (Matt. 4:8–10), he replied with another of these phrases, "Worship the Lord your God, and serve only him" (Deut. 6:13).

Jesus rooted himself clearly in the Ten Commandments. He was in the same tradition as Moses. There is continuity between the Old Testament and the New Testament, because there is continuity between Moses and Jesus. Jesus follows in the great tradition that is anti-Egypt and anti-empire, and remembers, "I am the LORD your God, who brought you out of the land of Egypt, out of the house of slavery." In the wilderness the tempter tried to enslave Jesus.

The kingdom of God

The priority of Jesus' message was the kingdom of God[1] (where kingdom is an almost identical word to empire). First and foremost, Jesus was interested in drawing people into God's different sort of empire. He did not seek to usurp Caesar's place as emperor or Christianise the Empire. He simply proclaimed the kingdom of God was the true way. His agenda was far greater than replacing a temporary earthly ruler.

When he was asked the trick question, "Is it lawful for us to pay taxes to the emperor, or not?" Jesus gave the unexpected answer, "Give to the emperor the things that are the emperor's, and to God the things that are God's" (Luke 20:20–26). He was not interested in taking over Caesar's power and role. The kingdom Jesus spoke about was completely different to anything that had been seen in human empires.

As well as his kingdom being an alternative way to Caesar's Rome, Jesus also opposed what he saw as oppressive and exploitative in Jewish society, especially the sin he saw manifested in the dominant temple system. He did not want to take over the running of the temple any more than he wanted to take over the Roman system, however. The kingdom of God was not to be brought about simply by reorganising structures or through brute force, but through suffering love.

Somebody asked me recently, "Does God have a plan for the world?" I immediately answered, "Yes, the kingdom of God." What God came to do and save in Jesus has to be understood in terms of the kingdom. When Jesus said, "The kingdom of God is at hand," God was unveiling the age-old plan that had been revealed in the deserts of Sinai. Jesus was not announcing a new or different plan or kingdom—it was the same one. As he began his work revealing God's kingdom, one might say, "At long last!" The return from exile, theologically and spiritually, was now finally happening in and through the ministry of Jesus.

The kingdom is mentioned over a hundred times in the Gospels. Jesus said it was near, that it belonged to the poor and the greatest one in it was like a child. He said it would embrace many people, including Abraham, Isaac and Jacob, those from the east and the west, and, surprisingly, tax collectors and prostitutes ahead of pious Jews. Jesus explained it with the images of farmers, treasure and yeast. He said our first priority in life must be to search out this kingdom. Jesus never stopped talking about the kingdom. If Jesus had spoken about sexual issues as often as this, we would have said he was obsessive.

In the kingdom, worldly values are turned upside down. The outsider is included and not exploited. The insider usually sees things the wrong way round and the poor have an advantage over those who are rich. In God's way of doing things, the king does not lord it over others, but behaves as a slave to them. In this empire women are taken seriously, debts are forgiven in good Sabbath style and the guilty are made clean.

In this new approach to living, we must abandon all our notions about power, position and prestige, because the categories our society values do not make sense. To live a kingdom-based life is to live a provocative life, as God's ways are not the world's ways.

The Beatitudes (Matthew 5:1–11)

If we are to live by the Ten Commandments, every generation must work out how they should be interpreted and implemented. As well as being very brief, they do not tell us what to do about so many of today's issues. They do not address stem-cell research, the ethics of the Internet or how the exploitation of the moon's resources should be managed, if at all. We have to do this work of interpretation ourselves.

The passage we often call the Sermon on the Mount (Matt. 5:1–7:29) is Jesus' interpretation of the Sinai commandments. He expands and fills them out saying, "Do not think that I have come to abolish the law or the prophets; I have come not to abolish but to fulfil" (Matt. 5:17). His teaching was, not surprisingly, a challenge to the way life was ordered, just as the original commandments were in contrast to the ways of Egypt.

Jesus' followers find out that living this other way is how they become "salt" and "light" (Matt. 5:13–16). This was the calling Israel had never fulfilled.

The Beatitudes are the profound sayings at the beginning of the Sermon on the Mount. They do not tell us what we should do; instead they tell us what we will be like if we live as kingdom people. The purpose of the Beatitudes, as with the Ten Commandments, is not to get us to comply with a set of regulations, but rather to urge us to become a certain sort of people. We may prefer they were laws to be kept, so that we could either accept them unquestioningly or rebel against them. It is easier to deal with boundaries rather than such openness. The Beatitudes, though, are wisdom sayings which are probably too mature for us most of the time:

> Blessed are the poor in spirit, for theirs
>> is the kingdom of heaven.
> Blessed are those who mourn, for they will be comforted.
> Blessed are the meek, for they will inherit the earth.
> Blessed are those who hunger and thirst for
>> righteousness, for they will be filled.
> Blessed are the merciful, for they will receive mercy.
> Blessed are the pure in heart, for they will see God.
> Blessed are the peacemakers, for they
>> will be called children of God.
> Blessed are those who are persecuted for righteousness'
>> sake, for theirs is the kingdom of heaven.
> Blessed are you when people revile you and
>> persecute you and utter all kinds of evil against
>> you falsely on my account. (Matt. 5:3–11)

These sayings are usually translated with the word "Blessed", as above. I have always felt this was a rather unhelpful translation of the original Greek word *makarioi*. It tends to give the Beatitudes a rather overly religious feel. Jesus did not mean these to be holy phrases. They are paradoxical and counter-cultural sayings. Christopher Jamison, in his book *Finding Happiness* uses the word "congratulations" instead of blessed. "Congratulations when you are merciful, for you will receive mercy." When I mentioned this in one of my sermons, a lady said to me at the end of the service as she was leaving, "I like that, but I prefer 'Well done!'" On refection, I do too. It captures the spirit of Jesus' teaching. "Well done, those who know they are spiritually poor, for theirs is the kingdom of heaven."

The Beatitudes express what is inconvenient for empires. Imperial regimes find it hard to deal with people who are humble and merciful to others. They cannot cope well with our mourning. They prefer us to "get over it" and "move on"; grief is inconvenient for the efficiency of empire. Jesus says well done for taking time to mourn as this is how you will find your healing. Empires do not find peacemakers easy to accommodate, as conciliators do not reach their solutions through dominative power.

We have heard the Beatitudes read so often that they have lost something of their sharpness and edge. They have become degraded and flattened; reduced and spiritualised for individual Christian piety. A little while ago I was pulled up rather sharply about this. I heard about a priest who was required to read out loud, as part of his seminary training, some excerpts from a Satanic version of the Beatitudes. He found that the brutality and violence of these words cast the original Beatitudes of Jesus in a completely new and refreshing light.

> Blessed are the Strong, for they shall possess the earth—Cursed are the weak for they shall inherit the yoke.
>
> Blessed are the Powerful for they shall be reverenced among men—Cursed are the Feeble for they shall be blotted out.
>
> Blessed are the Bold for they shall be masters of the world—Cursed are the Humble for they shall be trodden under hoofs.
>
> Blessed are the Victorious for victory is the basis of Right—Cursed are the vanquished for they shall be vassals for ever.
>
> Blessed are the battle-blooded, Beauty shall smile upon them—Cursed are the Poor in spirit, they shall be spat upon.
>
> Blessed are the audacious for they have imbibed true wisdom—Cursed are the Obedient for they shall breed Cripplings.
>
> Blessed are the iron handed, the unfit shall flee before them—Cursed are the haters of battle, subjugation is their portion.[2]

These are the values of empire. This is the spirit of Egypt, Babylon, Persia and Rome. This is the business of the global market and the ethos of the workplace for many today. What the nations do not understand is that true transformation can only be experienced through taking a different journey through life, where love and justice are the guiding values.

"The one who loses wins" is fundamental to the law of the gospel. Success has almost nothing to teach us in terms of the true wisdom of the kingdom. We can understand through losing. Our culture is all about success, however, which is where we wrongly believe wisdom lies. Jesus tells us freedom comes by letting go and living comes through dying. This is the paradoxical way of the kingdom of God, which is not just for individuals, but for communities too.

Jesus, Sinai and Sabbath

Jesus' ministry was thoroughly embedded in the tradition of the Ten Commandments and Moses. The kingdom he proclaimed was deeply rooted and integrated with the Old Testament story. His gospel was not a new or different story. Jesus demonstrated and proclaimed what Israel should have done centuries before. The age-old project of God was finally brought into being in and through Jesus.

He was a radical, in the truest sense of the word. He was getting back to Israel's roots, not in a simplistic or reactionary way, but according to the principles which God's people had pledged themselves to at Sinai—the Ten Commandments. Jesus said, "Do not think that I have come to abolish the law or the prophets; I have come not to abolish but to fulfil" (Matt. 5:17).

As far as Jesus was concerned, the commandments were as central as ever. He had not come to erode the demands of the law with some sort of permissive agenda. Jesus had come to intensify its importance. He was in the same tradition as the prophets who repeatedly drew the people's attention back to Sinai.

In the Sermon on the Mount, Jesus specifically highlights three of the Ten Commandments:

Murder

> You have heard that it was said to those of ancient times,
> "You shall not murder"; and "whoever murders shall be
> liable to judgement." But I say to you that if you are angry
> with a brother or sister, you will be liable to judgement;
> and if you insult a brother or sister, you will be liable to
> the council; and if you say, "You fool", you will be liable to
> the hell of fire. (Matt. 5:21–22)

Adultery

> You have heard that it was said, "You shall not commit
> adultery." But I say to you that everyone who looks at a
> woman with lust has already committed adultery with her
> in his heart. (Matt. 5:27–28)

Bearing false witness

> Again, you have heard that it was said to those of ancient
> times, "You shall not swear falsely, but carry out the vows
> you have made to the Lord." But I say to you, Do not swear
> at all, either by heaven, for it is the throne of God, or by
> the earth, for it is his footstool, or by Jerusalem, for it is the
> city of the great King. (Matt. 5.33–35)

Each time, Jesus begins with, "You have heard that it was said . . ." and
then goes on to say, "But I say to you . . ." In doing so he does not weaken
the commandments; he strengthens and expands them, making them
more demanding. He homes in on the motivation which lies behind
them. No one can escape by saying they did not "technically" break a
rule. Jesus reinforced the Law of Moses without in any way endorsing
or promoting legalism. Jesus' stance on the law was also applied to the
keeping of the Sabbath.

The Sabbath is mentioned more times in the Gospels than in the first five books of the Bible. It had become a very serious matter around the time of Jesus. Back in Jewish history, the violation of the Sabbath was one of Israel's most flagrant sins leading up to its national captivity (Jer. 17:21–22, 27; Ez. 20:12–13, 16). Once the exiles had returned and re-established themselves back in Jerusalem, they were determined never to make the same mistake again. Consequently, over the centuries that followed, the religious authorities over-legislated, defining in ever-increasing detail what could be done on the Sabbath and what could not be done. They were determined never to break this commandment ever again.

It was into this charged atmosphere, with its over-critical religious elite, that Jesus entered with his teachings and miracles. Today, we may sometimes feel he was rather lax in his approach to the law, but we could not be further from the truth. Jesus' intention was to restore the principle of the Sabbath and the rest of the commandments to their original purpose.

On the Sabbath, Jesus attended the synagogue, healed the sick and cast out demons. His compassion for the sick brought him into conflict with religious leaders. He understood, though, that the purpose of the Sabbath was to bring hope and renewal to humanity. Controversially, he allowed his disciples to pick grain as they passed through a field. Jesus was severely criticised for this. He had broken one of their miniscule regulations. For Jesus, though, his disciples were not harvesting the field; they were picking a few grains because they were hungry.

As far as Jesus was concerned, the Sabbath was made for the benefit of men and women as a time for rest from what usually happened on a working day. It was not about making sure petty rules were kept. So he said, "The Sabbath was made for humankind, and not humankind for the Sabbath; so the Son of Man is lord even of the Sabbath" (Mark 2:27–28).

Jesus did not change the law. He ignored the highly restrictive regulations imposed by the religious elite. He never broke God's commandments. Jesus was quite clear on this point: "I tell you, until heaven and earth pass away, not one letter, not one stroke of a letter, will pass from the law until all is accomplished" (Matt. 5:18).

In the Sermon on the Mount we have some of Jesus' clearest teachings. They are rooted in the laws of Sinai without being legalistic. As the commandments stood in contrast to the ways of Egypt, so Jesus' teaching countered the way life was ordered for most of Israel, and indeed the Roman Empire.

Much later in his ministry, Jesus was on another mountain where he was transfigured (Matt. 17:1–7). It was a sign to him, and his three closest disciples, that God was with them as Jesus faced his final and fateful journey into Jerusalem. Significantly, it was Moses and Elijah who appear alongside him in this visionary experience. Through this event Sinai was yet again reaffirmed, as Moses was present, and the prophets were reaffirmed, as Elijah was present. It was as if God was making the point as clear and loud as possible, that God's direction and calling of the Old Testament still stood.

A case study: the rich young man (Mark 10:17–31)

A rich young man came to Jesus and asked, "What must I do to inherit eternal life?" Jesus asked him if he knew the commandments. It was clear he did. He added he had kept these since he was young. Jesus commends him on this. The text says Jesus loved him, but then goes on to say, "You lack one thing; go, sell what you own, and give the money to the poor, and you will have treasure in heaven; then come, follow me" (Mark 10:21). Shocked, the man walked away grieving.

In those days you were regarded as having God's favour if you were wealthy. This explains why the disciples (who, relative to this man, were poor) exclaimed, "Who then can be saved?" Through this encounter, we learn Jesus was not asking this man to keep his riches and be a "spiritual" person. That sort of piety was not acceptable to Jesus. He was asking him to comply with the Ten Commandments. Here is how we know this.

In those days, land was the basis of wealth. This rich man must have had much property; he was one of a very small number of people in Israel (the elite) who owned land. The disciples admired him because he was so rich; he therefore must be blessed by God. Jesus focuses on how he became so rich, however. Wealth could be accumulated in a number of ways: by forming large estates, through arranged marriages and political alliances. The main way people became rich, though, was through the mechanism of debt.

Rather than being a wonderful example of an entrepreneur, the man's wealth most probably came from the poverty of others. This is how it worked. Tenant farmers would struggle to compete in the marketplace under the burden of taxes, rent and other tariffs. Large landowners could produce more crops and undercut the smaller operator. They also happened to be the agents the tenant farmers had to sell their produce to. The landowners were then able to buy at a price that was of benefit to them and not to the smallholder. In order to survive, these smallholders had to take out loans to make ends meet. There were no banks, as we have them today, so money had to be borrowed from those who had it—the rich landowners—at high rates of interest. As the burden of debts increased, the small operator found he could not service the loan. In time, their collateral (their land) was seized with the result the rich became even richer. This contravened so much of what was laid down in the law following Sinai, even down to not taking collateral against loans or charging a fellow Israelite interest.

Interestingly, Jesus mentions only a selection of the Ten Commandments to the rich man. He does not refer to the first four "religious" commands, just those that applied to one's neighbour (Mark 10:19), so that the he could not play at being a pious, religious Jew. Notice too, Jesus replaces the last commandment "Do not covet" with an alternative version from the book of Leviticus, "Do not defraud" (Lev. 19:13). The use of this alternative version leads us to understand that this rich man, like so many others Jesus saw, had built and maintained his wealth through fraud. His wealth was not a gift from God; it was gained through deceit. As this encounter unfolded it is almost as if we can hear the words from the prophet Isaiah again, "Woe to you who add house to house and join field to field till no space is left and you live alone in the land" (Isa. 5:8).

Instead of "Well done," Jesus tells him, "You lack one thing." Jesus is not inviting him to change his attitude to his money or to become a better boss. He did not ask him to become more committed in his faith. Jesus' answer to the question, "What must I do to inherit eternal life?" is to practise Jubilee: forgive debts, redistribute wealth and set people free.

In this conversation, Jesus exposed the system that gave the rich man privilege and asked him to restore to the poor what has been taken from them. This is how God's people are to live.

Power and the kingdom

Having considered some of Jesus' teachings, it is fair to ask if he was interested in power at all. How he related to power and how he handled it was so different to everyone else he met who had power. It seems to me that the Bible says the only story of power you can trust is the story of people who have journeyed into powerlessness or who have always been powerless. To many of us, this does not make sense. If we have money, property, education or a role in society; we have power, we have something to protect and defend. Those who have no power have nothing to defend.

Israel was chosen because they were nothing and, as desert nomads, had little or nothing. Later in the Old Testament story, Gideon was chosen to lead God's people. He was the least in his family, his family was the least in his clan, and his clan was the least of all the clans. In the New Testament Mary (a powerless, unknown young woman) is called to be the mother of Jesus.

In his enthronement sermon as Archbishop of Canterbury, Rowan Williams said:

> We must turn to the children; the exhausted; the ravaged and burdened and oppressed—they know the secret. Unless we know that we need life, we'll be baffled; but we hate admitting our lack, our poverty. It's the really hungry who can smell fresh bread a mile away. For those who know their need, God is immediate—not an idea, not a theory, but life, food, air for the stifled spirit and the beaten, despised, exploited body.[3]

In the kingdom it is only people who do not need power who can be safely trusted with power. Those who need power are usually the ones who cannot handle it with true justice. It is no surprise then that Jesus says we will not even enter the kingdom if we do not first become like a child. Children, of course, were one of the groups in the society of Jesus' day who had no power.

The disciples were not immune from the desire to have power. When walking to Capernaum, alongside Galilee, Jesus asked the disciples what they had been talking about (Mark 9:33–37). None of them would dare answer him because they had been talking about power. They were arguing about who was the greatest. They were interested in status, position and prestige.

Jesus roundly contradicted the social stratification of society. He saw it as one of the structures of evil in the world. He proclaimed a kingdom where such distinctions have no place and no meaning. So he said to his disciples, "Whoever wants to be first must be last of all and servant of all" (Mark 9:35). Then he held a child in his arms and pointed out that in welcoming such a lowly child in Jesus' name, one was welcoming the very life of God. Power in God's economy is quite a different entity to how power is usually practised in the world. It is the power of the powerless.

Jesus and women

The largest group of people who had little or no power in Jesus' day were women. Their status had not changed since Old Testament times. Women were not free people. They were under the control and ownership of either their fathers or their husbands. They could not own property; they were property, considered less than human. Denied an education and any rights, their lives were expendable. Only men could initiate a divorce. In a deeply patriarchal society women were mistreated, abused and exploited. It was a man's world. If you were a woman you had to find your place in their world—that is, until Jesus came.

When the Holy Spirit approached Mary to tell her she would conceive the Son of the Most High who would reign over an eternal kingdom (Luke 1:31–33), her father and fiancé were not consulted or asked to approve of this arrangement. It was Mary alone who said, "Let it be with me according to your word." Up to this point, no woman in Mary's family had been taken so seriously.

Throughout his ministry, Jesus challenged the conventional patriarchy of the societies he encountered, both Jewish and Gentile. Like the spirit of empire, patriarchy was never restricted to Jewish culture.

Jesus' ministry depended on women. They supported him financially, accompanied him on the road (Luke 8:1–3) and ministered to him (Luke 7:36–38). For any other man of his day, this would have been a matter of shame, but Jesus was not ashamed. He allowed women to sit at his feet and learn; traditionally the place of a male disciple and someone who aspired to be a rabbi. He opposed the double standard on divorce and gave women a voice.

In law, women were not considered reliable or rational enough to be witnesses, yet Jesus chose to appear to Mary Magdalene at his resurrection before any of his male disciples. He told her to go and be a witness to them about what had happened.

Jesus lived provocatively in a male-dominated society, taking the side of oppressed, abused and excluded women. He was part of that thin strand of Jewish tradition which allowed the inclusion of women like the prophet Hulda (2 Kings 22:14), Deborah the judge (Judges 4:4) and Esther the queen, who between them advised kings and priests, led Israel and saved the Jews from genocide. He took women seriously, just as he took children and all men seriously.

The temple (Luke 19:28–48)

If Jesus' encounter with the rich man is an example of how he confronted the spirit of empire in an individual, then his final visit to the temple is the illustration of how he dealt with empire at the heart of Israel.

The drama starts when Jesus enters the city at the beginning of the most important festival of the Jewish year—Passover (Mark 11:1–11). As it was the commemoration of the Exodus escape from empire, and, therefore, a possible rallying point for rebellion against Rome, the Roman governor, Pontius Pilate, also came to the city each year with troops ready to suppress any uprising. As he entered town, soldiers lined the streets with shields, spears and swords—demonstrations of power. There was a parade of dressed horses, part of the military equipment used by Rome. Then, at the rear of the procession, the governor rode on the smartest horse of the procession. This was the sort of power one should not mess with.

On the other side of town, Jesus staged an alternative street drama which ridiculed the governor's parade. He did not ride on a well-trained, magnificent horse, but on a donkey that had never been ridden before. There was no military escort or guards to keep people out of the way. Instead, there were people along the way who placed branches from the fields and clothes off their backs in the roadway as a carpet. These ordinary people shouted a royal salute, but not to Emperor Caesar. "Hosanna, God bless the king who comes in the name of the Lord," they sang as Jesus rode past. He came as a non-hero. This farce, or parody, mocked the Emperor, re-enacting what the prophet Zechariah had imagined possible so many centuries before: "Lo, your king comes to you; triumphant and victorious is he, humble and riding on a donkey" (Zech. 9:9–10). This is a demonstration not of the power of domination, but of humility.

As Jesus headed into the city he did not turn right into Herod's palace to unseat him as the local puppet king. He turned left, into the temple precincts. There he drove the merchants out of the courtyards. With zeal and anger he shouted, "It is written, 'My house shall be a house of prayer'; but you have made it a den of robbers" (Luke 19:46). His action was audacious. This is, of course, not a protest against selling postcards and perfumes at the back of church. It is not about stopping people paying a pound to come to a beetle drive in the nave of the church. It is clearly a much more important issue.

Jesus was furious because the religious elite were exploiting the poor; they had "fixed" the market. On the whole, the pilgrims who came to worship at the temple each year were poor. They were not allowed to bring animals from home to sacrifice; they had to buy them from the temple traders. Also, as it was a monopoly market, the prices were fixed. On top of all this, the pilgrims were forced to use the unscrupulous moneychangers of the temple in order to pay in the right currency. As a result, the religious elite of the temple became rich on the backs of the poor.

The problem was even more serious than this. The temple was not just a place of worship; it was the economic powerhouse of Jerusalem. It operated as the bank of Jerusalem and became the place which kept the record of the debts of the poor. The whole system was deceitful and corrupt.

Empires do not like their methods being unmasked and shown for what they are. Through his prophetic action, Jesus revealed that the temple operated as an imperial system. Cleansing the temple was part of his challenge to its system of domination and Israel's embrace of the spirit of empire. Those he unmasked saw his action as blasphemy against the doctrine of "business as usual".

Throughout his ministry, Jesus unmasked injustice wherever he saw it. Eventually, neither the systems of empire within the temple nor the Romans could accommodate Jesus any longer, so together they conspired to kill him.

At the heart of Israel there was supposed to be the dynamic, radical freedom of God, bringing his life-giving way rather than the life-denying way of empire. But Jesus saw the temple as an oppressive institution which had sold out to the ways of the "nations". He believed it had no part in God's plan. Jesus saw that he himself would replace the temple and he foretold its demise and destruction. Then, in AD 70, it was destroyed and has never been replaced since.

With the cleansing of the temple, Jesus took upon himself, not its administration, but its mission and authority. It is in this sense that Jesus replaced the temple.

Exodus again: the last supper (Matthew 26:26–30 & John 13:1–17)

At the festival of Passover, Jesus and his disciples, like all good Jews, remembered the very first Exodus of their people from the slavery of Egypt. But this Passover meal was to be different. This time they did not eat the "bread of affliction" (Deut. 16:3) as they had always done before. Instead, Jesus put himself in its place when he passed the bread around, by saying, "Take, eat, this is my body," and then when he gave the cup saying, "Drink from it, all of you; for this is my blood of the covenant" (Matt. 26:26–27). Then he declared the long spiritual exile of Israel was ending and the kingdom was about to come: "I tell you, I will never again drink of this fruit of the vine until that day when I drink it new with you in my Father's kingdom" (Matt. 26:29). Here, in Jesus, God's people are being led out of slavery, once again to enjoy the way of life God had always intended for humanity. Jesus calls his disciples to come and follow him and establish the empire of God: not with the weapons of violence, oppression and worldly power, but with love.

The occasion of the washing of feet at this Passover meal is sometimes portrayed as a task that Jesus should not really have done, because it was a messy job more suited to slaves. Today, it is acted out at many Maundy Thursday services in churches and cathedrals with clean towels and warm, soapy water. It is used to illustrate Jesus was a servant and we should be too. This is good, but I believe what happened in that Upper Room stands for something even more powerful than this.

When Jesus took the place of the house-slave on this Thursday evening, it was not just a bit embarrassing for Peter and the other disciples; it was a shameful thing for them to be a part of. Peter's reaction is not one of mild discomfort or embarrassment with the roles being played out here; he is horrified. He steadfastly refuses to let Jesus wash his feet. If he is really going to do some washing, then it really must not be just the feet, but his entire body. Why such a strong reaction?

We have to understand something of the etiquette of Middle Eastern culture. In Jesus' day, and it is still very much true today, the feet were considered the lowliest and the most shameful parts of the body. In 2003, when the victorious coalition troops entered Bagdad, the statue of Saddam

Hussein in Firdos Square was pulled down in front of hundreds of Iraqis. The images were broadcast all over the world. As soon as the statue hit the ground it was interesting to see what the local people did to it. They hit it with the soles of their shoes and feet. This was the ultimate insult to a ruler who had oppressed them. I learnt in Birmingham, living in a predominantly Muslim neighbourhood, that I should not sit in someone's home or in a mosque with the soles of my feet pointing outwards towards other people. Not only was it impolite, it was rude.

The insult of the feet is so bad because they are viewed as carrying shame. We, today, would feel shame if somebody exposed their genitals in public. Maybe the greatest act of shame in our culture would be for someone to urinate on somebody else, or on something important. Not long ago a student in Southampton, who came from where I lived at that time, Macclesfield, was photographed urinating on the cenotaph memorial while out on a drunken pub crawl. The press then got hold of the story. It was rightly regarded across town as an act of the greatest disrespect.

When Jesus put himself in the position of a foot-washing slave, he was voluntarily accepting great shame. There is much more to this action than washing hot and smelly feet in a dusty environment. Jesus was shaming himself and Peter was shamed because the action was done to him. Peter could not handle it, but Jesus could.

Ernest Becker, in his book *The Denial of Death*, says we seek to live heroic lives because we cannot cope with the possibility of shame. If we can be successful and applauded in life, then we will not be looked down on. Our shame can be so unbearable that some people would rather die than face it.

In 2009, a terrible example of this hit the news. Because of the shame of the financial mess the millionaire Christopher Foster had got himself and his family into, he murdered his wife and fifteen-year-old daughter. He then shot their pet dogs and horses and set his £1.2 million mansion ablaze before committing suicide himself. He just could not face his shame. He chose to end it all instead.

Jesus' action in the Cenacle (the "Upper Room") was a significant action. Not only did he demonstrate he was a servant king, but also that he could handle anything we might regard as an attack on our pride, self-respect or ego. If Jesus was a king or emperor, then he was a very different one from those we see in the world as monarchs, dictators, CEOs, politicians or leaders, inside or outside of the church. If Jesus the King is not offended or reduced in stature by such shame, then his kingdom is also a very different way of living from what we are used to in the world. This act of coping with shame prepares Jesus for his greatest shame, dying on the cross—a criminal's execution.

Jesus directs his disciples not to be afraid of shame by saying, "So if I, your Lord and Teacher, have washed your feet, you also ought to wash one another's feet" (John 13:14).

The cross

The cross of Jesus stands at the heart of all that Christians believe. It has become the icon and symbol of our faith. Sadly, it has been used in imperial ways: on the shields of crusaders, to stand out over other religious symbols and remains to this day on the flags of many nations, including our own.

The original Roman cross was a method of execution which maximised pain and shame. The cross of Christ demonstrates that God stands with us through the pain of suffering love. What we believe about the cross, its doctrine, helps us to understand everything—if we get it right. The crucifixion of Jesus, with his passion and suffering and his raising up from death, helps us to interpret the entire Bible, and indeed all of history. What we have seen hinted at in the history of the Old Testament, we now see more clearly in the cross of Jesus.

The story of the Bible so far has taught us that empires have no time for weakness, suffering or vulnerability. They believe in power and strength. Enemies have to be defeated or excluded, as they are a threat to the status quo. Throughout history, human institutions and societies have sought to deal with evil by means of sacrificial systems rather than forgiveness. If something has gone wrong or some evil has been done, they believe somebody must suffer or even die to pay for it. Then, if an individual was blamed, punished, imprisoned or killed, it is believed some good had been achieved; that there had been a degree of redemption. Evil is not reduced or diffused in this way, however—it is multiplied.

This dynamic still happens today. If we hear on the news that a great mistake has been made or accident occurred, the public tends to feel some degree of redemption will have resulted if a government minister, a CEO, a head of a statutory organisation or some other prominent person is sacked or forced to resign. Some may say, though, in defence of the humiliated person, that they have just been made a "scapegoat" for everyone else. This is an ancient Old Testament tradition (Lev. 16:20–22). But Jesus establishes, once and for all, a way to deal with evil, sin and shame; not by violence of any sort or by "scapegoating", but through forgiveness. By his action on the cross he has effectively said, "If you need somebody to suffer and be killed for all evil and sin, then let me be the last and final victim." Jesus stands, or rather hangs, as the ultimate victim of this violence and, being innocent, as the most powerful act of forgiveness.

Over the centuries, Christians have had different ideas about who was being "paid off" in this horrendous transaction. In the early centuries, it was thought the Devil had to be paid off to put an end to all this evil. Then, in the eleventh century, it was thought that maybe this debt had to be paid to God the Father. We are now starting to realise that the debt was being paid to us. It is we who require somebody should be blamed and made to suffer for all that has gone wrong. Jesus died for our sake, because we needed a victim. It was we who demanded a death, as all people with an imperial mind-set do. Jesus, though, with an anti-imperial mind-set, refused to play the blame game or deal with the problem of evil by violence. He defeated evil with suffering love.

If we do not deal with evil and sin this way, we will always end up passing it on to others. Jesus absorbed it into himself and became the eternal sacrifice. We are called away from "the nations" because they do not believe this. God's people are called to model this way of living, by absorbing evil themselves, and so become a light to "the nations". Rome and Israel killed Jesus together. The Sanhedrin, the highest court of justice, and the supreme council in ancient Jerusalem, realised they did not have the legal right to execute him themselves, so they asked Rome to do it on the basis that Jesus was a rival to the Emperor. The Romans knew a rival could not be tolerated, and so Jesus had to be eliminated.

It is important to note here that the Jews did not kill Jesus. The system they were enslaved by demanded he should die. It was imperial power that killed him.

The resurrection

Initially, the empire got a momentary sniff of victory because Jesus had chosen the way that looks like failure and death. Empires are not programmed to see there could be something positive about the position of weakness. They did not see Jesus was following life, not death. From the empire's point of view it all appeared to be the wrong way round. It is hard to see what happened over those three days of Easter as a victory for anyone apart from the religious establishment and Rome. God had not put in place a heroic movie star. For generations, God's people had prayed for a Messiah, a superhero type figure, who would come with power and glory, overthrow the pagans who ruled over them and rule as a potent king. Instead, they were given a baby lying in straw who, when he grew up, did not overthrow the Romans but instead let himself be crucified by them.

The cross and resurrection teach us that God does not intervene in the world to stop death and suffering by brutal force. Peace cannot come through violence (despite what our politicians tell us) and reconciliation does not result from war. Rather, Jesus redeems pain and overcomes death by entering into it.

The resurrection vindicated Jesus' way of being a king. What he did may have looked strange, weak, subversive and weirdly alternative, but his rising from death proved that we do not have to continually put up with empire as the only way to live in this world. The resurrection established, once and for all, that the powers, shaped and constructed by the nations, were not to be given worth or space—but Jesus was. Even if Rome said, "Caesar is Lord," it was now clear this was untrue, as "Jesus is Lord." The resurrection vindicated the kingdom of God, based on the commandments of Sinai, as being the empire which brings life, love and justice.

This dramatic and central event of the Christian faith is not to be left in the closet of history as something that happened as a one-off affair. Jesus teaches us to take up our cross daily and follow him, and that we find our life by losing it and we lose our life by trying to hang on to it.

The death and resurrection of Jesus are not to remain part of a nice theory to be remembered in church services and discussed in theological colleges. These events represent the way to live life every day. As I have already said, it is through dying that we live and through losing that we find. Resurrection is what happens when we take the other path through life, as we give room for God to act in our lives and in the world.

In Jesus we see the principles of Sinai and Sabbath affirmed and demonstrated. Through the way he acted, he restored neighbourliness. He declared the time of exile had ended and restoration had begun. Through resurrection, he showed the alternative path to the way of empire and violence. He did what Israel failed to do. He did not give into the seduction of empire and its "easy" power. Jesus "did it right", and called a group of disparate women and men to do the same. This was the beginning of the church.

Questions for discussion

1. What are the "empires" that seek to dominate our lives that we need to stand against and say, "No, Jesus is Saviour of the World"?

2. What have the Western allies claimed about bringing peace in Iraq, Afghanistan and Middle East countries through military intervention? What do the birth narratives of Jesus have to say to us about this?

3. How do we encounter desert experiences today? As individual Christians? As church communities? As nations/cultures? Desert places have always been linked with the training of the soul and spiritual maturity. What have "desert places" to teach us in our churches today?

4. The priority of Jesus' message was to draw people into a different sort of empire, the kingdom of God. What sort of kingdom does your church speak about? In what ways is the church tempted back into the ways of empire?

5. What did you feel when you read the excerpt from the Satanic Beatitudes quoted in this chapter? How can Jesus' Beatitudes become a radical charter for the church today?

Prayer

O Son of Mary;
    help us to remember that we are
    light-bearers for all people
    and for all creation,
    until you return
    to make all things new.
May we be as unthreatening
    to the poor and disadvantaged
    as a child in a manger,
but as subversive
    to the rich and powerful
    as a man hanging on a cross.
And now may the Lord bless all people
    by ridding us of tyranny,
    by freeing us of debt,
    and by the gift of his divine presence,
    now and for evermore.
Amen.

Notes

1.   Matthew's Gospel refers to the kingdom of God as the "kingdom of heaven".
     Being a Gospel originally written for a largely Jewish audience the name "God"
     was avoided in order to fulfil the third commandment not to take the Lord's
     name in vain; Matthew avoided using the sacred name.

2.   <https://archive.org/stream/MightIsRight_966/MightIsRight#page/n27/
     mode/2up/search/blessed>.

3.   <http://rowanwilliams.archbishopofcanterbury.org/articles.php/1624/
     enthronement-sermon>.

CHAPTER 9

The Early Believers

Most people find the Gospels easier to deal with than the letters that make up much of the New Testament. Paul's letters can be particularly difficult. Some of his tortuous arguments about righteousness and circumcision, or the on-going issues that crop up in the lives of these early Christian communities about church order, leave many people rather bewildered or even cold. In order to try and make sense of these passages we often resort to dealing with them as if they primarily address our separate, private lives. We do not read them as if they also address the contemporary political contexts of empire and kingdom I am covering in this book. As a result we over-spiritualise these texts, applying them, in the main, to the individual believer. This is a very restrictive reading of these books, however.

The Acts of the Apostles is a companion volume to Luke's first work, his Gospel. Taking these two books together helps us see Jesus' ministry and the work of the early church as a continuous whole. The book of Acts is not a separate new departure. If anything, it intensifies the prophetic nature of many passages such as Jesus' "manifesto statement" (Luke 4:16–30) and Luke's version of the Sermon on the Mount (Luke 6:17–36). Luke shows us that Paul and the early believers were interested in contemporary political realities as well as how the gospel applied to each person.

The church today struggles to pay attention to the imperial context of Paul's ministry and mission. In both of his books, Luke is passionate that the repentance Jesus proclaims is about the liberation of all people at a personal level and at the level of the systems and structures within which we all live. One theologian put it this way:

> The forgiveness of sins in Luke-Acts is neither a program of institutional reform nor a matter of private piety: it is the reformation of human politics that begins in the human heart and is expressed above all in an intentional community filled with and led by the Holy Spirit.[1]

It is the task of local Christian communities, the churches, to demonstrate God's alternative way of living, the kingdom of God, so the poor are lifted up, outsiders included, possessions shared, sins forgiven and leadership is marked by servanthood. It is not the task of the churches to lead a revolt against state authorities, although sometimes determined non-violent resistance will be required. For Luke, the way of Jesus was not necessarily contrary to the rule of Rome, although it often was in practice. The early Christians were told not to rebel against Rome, even if at times it made martyrs of some of them; neither were they told to acquiesce and be passive.

The church has a role in society to call to account those who govern over us and manage the businesses that dominate our lives. At the same time we should proclaim clearly and loudly that there is another king who is non-violent in all he does. The church does not seek to dethrone Caesar, but acknowledges ultimately its allegiance lies elsewhere.

The tradition of Abraham and Moses

All through Jesus' ministry, until the death of Judas, there had been the twelve disciples who symbolised the twelve tribes of Israel. Then, at the beginning of the book of Acts, having lost Judas, there was a clear sense among the wider group of believers there should be twelve disciples again; eleven just would not do (Acts 1:21–22). If they saw themselves as the true guardians of Israel then there had to be twelve (Acts 1:6). As a result, they appointed Matthias. In the following chapter, the gift of the Holy Spirit to the twelve (now called apostles) was to be a gift to Israel, so it could play its part in fulfilling the initial call to Abraham and Moses. The call to Abraham was to come out of Babylon and allow God to make him great in the way that God understands greatness. The call to Moses was to lead his people out of slavery and the ways of empire into an alternative way of living, based on the Ten Commandments, not rooted in exploitative and dehumanising practices.

Peter referred back to these two great figures of Jewish history. In his temple precincts speech (Acts 3:11–26), Peter appealed to Moses whom he said was talking about Jesus:

> Moses said, "The Lord your God will raise up for you from your own people a prophet like me. You must listen to whatever he tells you." (Acts 3:22)

He also affirmed the promise made to Abraham:

> You are the descendants of the prophets and of the covenant that God gave to your ancestors, saying to Abraham, "And in your descendants all the families of the earth shall be blessed." (Acts 3:25)

All that was promised and given to Abraham and Moses was still true for the Jewish people scattered throughout the temple courtyard at that Pentecost festival.

Stephen's speech is even more robust (Acts 7:1–53). It is his defence before the Council of Jerusalem. Bribed men had made false accusations against him. In his defiant defence he repeatedly appealed to Abraham and Moses while being completely respectful to the Council, calling them "brothers and fathers". Stephen was no rebel, but he was bold and determined. Like Peter, he also said Moses was speaking of Jesus:

> God will raise up a prophet for you from your own people as he raised me up. (Acts 7:37)

What Stephen said was too much for the Council to bear. They dragged him out of the city and stoned him to death. The text says Saul (also called Paul) approved of his murder (Acts 8:1). He too could not see the plan of God brought into being with Abraham and Sarah, made explicit with Moses and the Ten Commandments, and seen in Jesus of Nazareth. The spirit of empire was still strong among the Jewish people and their council in Jerusalem.

Pentecost: antidote to Babel (Acts 2:1–13)

Earlier, when we looked at the story of Babel, I explained that the people were scared of becoming insignificant and, therefore, attempted to "make a name for themselves" by constructing a large tower. They believed this would help them look powerful in the eyes of others and be in control of their own destiny. This is the impulse of empire: to build up, centralise and dominate. Babel is a story about the Babylonian empire. Here, at the beginning of the Acts of the Apostles, God's people lived under the domination of the Roman Empire, just as Jesus did. It had one imperial language—Greek. While the Jews would have spoken their own Aramaic language among themselves, they also had to communicate beyond family and community in the dominant Greek language.

On the feast of Pentecost (fifty days after Passover), the twelve apostles and many of the believers were gathered together in Jerusalem. The Holy Spirit came as a wind with what looked like "divided tongues, as of fire" resting on everyone. Immediately, they all began to speak in other languages "as the Spirit gave them ability". This is opposite to the impulse of empire, which tends to impose a single language, as at Babel. Here, the variety of languages was God-given. To emphasise and reinforce the point, Luke lists the many groups who heard their own particular language being spoken. They were all amazed and confused; they asked each other, "What does this mean?" The answer is this: God wants people to live in diversity as originally intended, a point that was made clear at the end of the story of Babel.

Rabbi Jonathan Sacks, from his perspective, affirms that God loves difference.[2] One of the great crimes of humanity is the dislike of those who are not similar to us. Sacks says God called the Jews to be different, as a sign that everyone can be different. What stood out about the Jews throughout history was the belief they had a right and a duty to live another way. Throughout history, Jews have generally resisted assimilation into the imperial culture or conversion to the dominant religion. God does not want us all to be alike. He loves the variety of languages, cultures, colours and traditions; this is where God is to be found.

At Pentecost, the first sign of the Spirit was linguistic diversity. This stood out against the uniformity of a monoculture and a single language: symptoms of imperial and economic domination. Pentecost was not just an efficient and effective way of communicating a message with a wide variety of people all at once; it was also about the restoration of God's order in the world. It was a sign of how God wanted things to be. A multiplicity of languages is a hedge against the primal instinct of one group to dominate, a characteristic of our human fallenness. A dominant language is a form of dominant power.

Jubilee at Pentecost

The second sign of the Spirit was social justice. It is significant that the Jewish festival of Pentecost (called the Feast of Weeks in the Old Testament) occurred fifty days after Passover. You will remember from our studies in the Old Testament that Israel had social practices that prevented the ways of empire re-establishing themselves. One of these happened every fiftieth year at the Jubilee festival. At this festival there was to be a general redistribution of the land. It reminded people the land belonged to God, and not to them. It prevented some from becoming permanently rich and ensured an underclass of poor people did not develop. This was how the economy was to work in God's way of doing things.

In Acts 2, the link between Pentecost and Jubilee was reinforced. As well as being the day when the Holy Spirit was given, it was the day when the principles of Jubilee were put into action. We read that as Peter addressed the gathered crowd, many heard their own native language being spoken. Some were "amazed and perplexed". Others were cynical, saying, "They are filled with new wine". When Peter finished addressing the large crowd, many were deeply moved. About three thousand people changed their thinking (i.e. repented), were baptised and joined the believers in following the teachings of the apostles. Numerous signs and wonders happened. Towards the end of the chapter, Luke states:

> All who believed were together and had all things in common; they would sell their possessions and goods and distribute the proceeds to all, as any had need. (Acts 2:44–45)

The events of this mighty day caused the believers to share their possessions. This is often understood to have happened because of the believers' increased sense of compassion towards other people as a result of turning to follow Jesus. This was not just simply an act of kindness and generosity, however; it was more than this. It was the community of Jewish believers enacting the principle of Jubilee (Lev. 25:13) on the day of Jubilee. They were Jews being obedient to God and the law by redistributing their wealth. Because of this, there was economic justice in the community. These people were not only moved; they were also obeying Old Testament Jubilee instructions.

Early in both of his volumes, Luke puts a marker down that makes it clear what the kingdom of God is about. In both Jesus' "manifesto statement" (Luke 4:18–19) and the coming of the Spirit at Pentecost (Acts 2), the Spirit was announced in the context of Jubilee. The coming of the Holy Spirit is not just an experience in the life of an individual believer. The coming of the Spirit brings in God's new age in such a way that everything is changed and affected, including the economy. The life of the Spirit in the church demands that we take Sinai seriously, not just in our relationship to God, but in how we relate to each other, especially economically.

Paul's experience on the Damascus Road (Acts 9:1–22)

Some years ago I ran a series of forty-minute Bible studies for a few women who did not want the men in their life to know they were interested in God. During a discussion about Acts 9, one of the women said, "I would love to have a conversion experience just like St Paul's." I blurted out, rather insensitively, "Oh no you wouldn't!" I think her comment contains two misunderstandings.

First, the Bible does not teach us that Paul (or Saul) was converted. The term is never used of him in the Bible (except in the sub-headings inserted by our contemporary editors and publishers). Also, conversion implies being converted *from* something. Paul was not converted from Judaism to Christianity. He was born a Jew, lived a Jew and died a Jew—he would not have understood his life any other way. Christianity, as such, did not exist. The term "Christian" was used of the early believers in the book of Acts by people outside of the community of faith, and used in a pejorative sense. We have grown up, though, with the idea that Paul converted to Christianity. Even though the idea is dominant throughout history in literature and art, it simply is not true. Paul never saw himself as anything but a Jew. On the road to Damascus, Paul was not converted; he was enlightened. He came to understand that Jesus brought fulfilment and wholeness to Judaism. He was not an "ex-Jew".

Our idea that Paul was converted to Christianity probably reflects our rather imperious notion that Paul became "one of us". The only people referred to as converts in the book of Acts were Gentiles, and the understanding was that they had converted to Judaism, not Christianity. At Pentecost, those who heard the believers speaking were both Jews and converts to Judaism (Acts 2:10; see also 6:5, 13:43, 15:3). These believers regarded themselves as Jews, albeit Jews who now believed Jesus was God and king. If Paul was a convert at all, it was from the bully-boy ways of the temple authorities to the way of Jesus; from violence to grace; from fear to love.

Second, I do not believe Paul's experience on the Damascus road was a pleasant one. I understand what my study group member was getting at: she wanted a clear decisive moment in her journey of faith that she could look back to in times of difficulty and doubt. What happened to

Paul, though, was a truly devastating event. It dismantled so much of what he had previously given his life to. Up to this point, Paul believed passionately that the Jews who followed Jesus were dangerous heretics. Not only that, they were also polluting and corrupting Judaism. As such, they deserved death. Paul's zealousness for his faith drove him to hunt down and kill these new believers, operating with a ruthlessness similar to the Taliban in Afghanistan and Pakistan.

Then, suddenly, on the road to Damascus, when he was confronted with the reality of who Jesus was, Paul had to face the fact that he had been imprisoning and putting to death innocent people. Not only that, but when he thought he had been protecting the faith of God's people, he had actually been killing them. In the one phrase, "Saul, Saul, why do you persecute me?" the awful truth dawned on him. He thought he had been attacking God's enemies. Now he realised he had been persecuting his people. To kill somebody accidently must be a bad enough experience. To intentionally kill people, when you believed what you were doing was right but then find out you were wrong, must be completely devastating. In this one moment, Paul's life came crashing down round him. In the language of spirituality we call this the death of the ego, or the False Self. Paul had over-identified with his role, with who he *thought* he was. When the life he had built crumbled around him, he had to face who he really was—a child of God, loved by God. His encounter with Jesus revealed to him what was real. What happened to Paul on the way to Damascus was that the spirit of empire within his life was demolished. Only then was he able to become a servant in the true empire, the kingdom of God.

Luke believed the transformation which happened in Paul's life on the way to Damascus was so important that he included it three times in the book of Acts (9:1–18, 22:6–16 and 26:12–18). Because of this dramatic event, the spiritual and political vision of Paul became rooted in the risen Jesus.

Two theological principles come out of the Damascus road experience for me. First, the ego has to die for the life of Christ to come alive in us. This is counter-cultural. It was in Paul's day, and it is today. Our cultural assumptions are based on increase; that we need more: more possessions, more control, more acclaim, even more religion or spirituality. Empire believes that less is bad, and more is good. In God's economy, to live one has to die; to be rich one must become poor; to find one has to lose; to keep life one has to first lose it. Paul lost all he had and found everything. This anti-imperial paradox has to be embraced to be understood.

The second principle is that the people of God are the body of Christ. What must have confused Paul initially was the Lord's phrase, "Why do you persecute *me*?" Clearly, he did not think he was hunting God down; just these errant Jews. My guess is that he meditated on this for a long time as he tried to understand what it meant. I like to think his extended retreat in Arabia, as he reassessed his life after the Damascus road event, was centred on this one phrase. In any case, from this came one of Paul's most important theologies—the believers as "the body of Christ". They were not just people who believed in Jesus, they actually *were* his presence here in the world—his body, his life, his being. Not only that, they also participated mystically in the life of Christ. Thus Paul repeatedly used the term "in Christ".

In the kingdom of God, its people are not merely subjects of the king to be used and exploited, as they were in the empires. In God's way of doing things, the people of the kingdom participate in the very life of the king, with all the benefits and privileges.

The cult of Caesar

Paul was not only born a Jew, he was also born a Roman. He tells us he came from the important city of Tarsus situated in what we now call south-eastern Turkey. He was deeply immersed in the culture of the Roman Empire. Like nearly all the people of God throughout history, Paul had to live in two worlds: the world of the empire and the world of his faith. Because of this, Paul, like Daniel and his friends, had two names. He had the Hebrew name Saul, given to him by his family, and the Greek name Paul, from the empire. Paul/Saul had to learn to live with a dual identity. He had to learn how to be "bilingual" (in faith and empire), to work out how much he could accommodate and compromise. He had to decide when to live quietly in empire and when to resist its power and seduction.

We live with the same tension today. It is the same tension people of faith have always lived with. My fear is we have compromised and accommodated far too much, just as other Christians have over the centuries. To resolve this tension, some people have completely opted out of empire, forming quite separate communities or communes from the rest of society. Paul did not do this. He, like many before him, chose to learn to negotiate living between faith and empire. Today, Christians who are more conservatively inclined in their faith tend towards separation. Those who are more liberally inclined tend to feel happier about throwing their lot in with the empires of the day. I believe we are called to stand in the (often painful) gap between the two approaches and learn how to find a way of living there.

A few decades before the birth of Jesus, a series of violent civil wars led to the demise of the Roman Republic. In its dying days, Julius Caesar became ruler and was given the name *Dictator perpetuo* (dictator in perpetuity). Power was centralised in Rome and in the ruler. Following his assassination and the transitional Second Triumverate, his adopted son, Octavius, received the name Augustus and became the first Roman emperor. The era of the Empire began with a vengeance.

In time, a cult grew up, more or less spontaneously around the emperor. He became more than a political head of state; he became a divine figure. Temples were built and dedicated to him. Festivals were celebrated in his honour and on behalf of his family. Prayers were said, sacrifices made, and games played on these auspicious occasions.

By the time of Paul, this had become the dominant cult across much of the empire. It enabled the emperor to control the populace. Everybody had some understanding of the cult of Caesar and the doctrine that accompanied it. You could not get through a single day without being aware of its promotional propaganda. Images and messages in public places reinforced it. Nobody could claim they did not know. The hype proclaimed that Caesar had brought peace (*Pax Romana*), but it was a peace imposed by military might and domination. The power of Rome was based on his imperial divinity, the strength of the Roman army and the economic power of the Roman currency. Ultimately, Caesar maintained peace through terror and violence. Because he had provided "justice" and "peace" to the known world, he was hailed as Lord and trusted as a Saviour.

Such cults were not new. They went right back to the days of the Babylonians. They are also characteristic of the empires of more recent times. For instance, from the mid-1920s in the Soviet Union, a personality cult developed around Joseph Stalin. Hymns were sung to him by vast choirs thanking him for his provision and praising him for his wisdom. Songs proclaimed that everything belonged to Stalin; that he brought life into being and made the blooms of spring happen. They affirmed there had never been anyone like him in the world before. The cult surrounding Stalin sounds so much like the cult of Caesar during the time of the early church.

Paul, however, announced that Jesus, the Jewish Messiah, was Lord and Saviour, not Caesar. At the beginning of so many of his letters, he talked about a peace which originates "from God our Father and from the Lord Jesus Christ"; not from Caesar. Significantly, Paul talked the most about this peace in his letter to the church at Rome. If the cult of Caesar is not compatible with faith in the risen Lord Jesus Christ, then the big question was, "How does one live as a believer, in the Roman Empire, when Jesus is Lord?" If Paul, together with the leaders of the early church, did not advocate revolt, then what sort of kingdom was it they were looking for in the risen Lord Jesus Christ?

Jesus is Lord and King

The main challenge for the early church was that their members might be seduced, not by a variety of pagan gods, but by the cult of Caesar. The message that Caesar's Rome had executed Jesus and therefore had power over him was quite overwhelming. Surely it had been established Caesar was lord of lords? The religion of Caesar dominated all other religions and absorbed them into its cult: the emperor should be hailed as Lord and trusted as Saviour. Paul saw things differently, though. He said, "If you confess with your lips that Jesus is Lord and believe in your heart that God raised him from the dead, you will be saved" (Rom. 10:9). We, however, are so used to the phrase "Jesus is Lord" being used within church circles rather than out in the political arena. We regard it as a religious statement usually confined to songs, hymns, liturgies and sermons. For Paul, it affirmed that Jesus was the one who was chief over the entire world; not Caesar with his empire, even though the empire seemed indomitable. Paul preached that it was not a human with mighty power who ruled the world, but a man who had hung on a cross in vulnerability, then rose and ascended. This was a radically new way of thinking. It challenged people, calling them to a new allegiance. The term "Jesus is Lord" then became a mantra of resistance and protest against the cult of Caesar. Peter made the same affirmation in his sermon at Pentecost when he declared, "God has made him both Lord and Messiah" (Acts 2:36).

In the prominent city of Thessalonica, a dangerous situation arose when Paul and Silas, together with the local believers, were accused of turning the Roman world upside down (Acts 17:1–9). They were charged with acting against the decrees of Caesar, because they said that there was *another* king, whose name was Jesus (Acts 17:7). There was a riot in the city. The local authority had to intervene to calm things down and sort it out. Like Peter, Paul and Silas spoke of a rival to Caesar. They did not mean that this new rival was set to usurp the throne of Caesar in some sort of coup d'état, though. Jesus, the true king, was a threat, but not in the way many would expect. There was no call for the people of God to lead a revolt.

As things stood, the power of the cult of Caesar was so great that it was clearly risky and dangerous to say there was another king. As a result, many Jews (both those who believed Jesus and those who did not) went along with the status quo and generally accepted that the Roman Empire as the dominant reality. Paul, along with other early church leaders, was not content to do this; his allegiance was to Jesus, not Caesar. Philippians 2:5–11 is an old liturgical hymn that was sung as a song of resistance. It stood defiantly against the cult of Caesar, or any other leadership cult for that matter, and presented Jesus as a quite different sort of king. One can almost hear interjections from off stage as the hymn was sung:

Let the same mind be in you that was in Christ Jesus,
"Do not adopt Caesar's way of thinking!"

> who, though he was in the form of God, did not regard
> equality with God as something to be exploited,
>> *"Unlike Caesar!"*
> but emptied himself, taking the form of a slave,
>> *"Which Caesar never did!"*
> being born in human likeness. And being found
> in human form, he humbled himself
>> *"Caesar never humbled himself!"*
> and became obedient to the point of
> death—even death on a cross.
>> *"Caesar never became obedient!"*
> Therefore God also highly exalted him
>> *"Whereas Caesar exalted himself!"*
> and gave him the name that is above every name,
>> *"Caesar is not the highest name!"*
> so that at the name of Jesus
>> *"Not at Caesar's name!"*
> every knee should bend,
>> *"Including all Romans, and even the Emperor!"*
> in heaven and on earth and under the earth,
>> *"In and beyond the Roman world!"*
> and every tongue should confess
>> *"Including all Romans, and even the Emperor!"*
> that Jesus Christ is Lord,
>> *"Caesar is not Lord!"*
> to the glory of God the Father.

Another hymn in the letter to the Colossians served the same purpose (Col. 1:15–20). By regularly singing these words, the early Christians affirmed their belief in another way of seeing the world, while still living in the empire where the propaganda was strong and persuasive. In liturgies like these, they declared that Jesus was the image of the invisible God, the firstborn of all creation, that all things had been created through him and for him, and that through Jesus, God was reconciling everything in the universe to himself. One did not sing these things lightly. If you were discovered doing so, you would pay a terrible price.

Paul's answer to Caesar's cult and empire was the empire of Jesus, the kingdom of God. This royal theme continues throughout the New Testament. Luke made reference to the kingdom right up to the end of his second volume. He tells us the kingdom is rooted in Jesus and the law of Moses, together with the prophets (Acts 28:23). From Abraham through to the end of the Bible, all humanity is called to a different way of living which is not "like the nations", whether they be the Babylonians, the Egyptians, the Romans or the powerful nations, cultures and corporations of our own day. It is no wonder there was a riot in Thessalonica. The people of the city were right; the believers were a threat to the way things were, religiously, economically and politically. They said there was another king. If this was not to lead to an uprising, then how were the Christians to relate to the empire? We now turn to consider this.

"Be subject to the governing authorities"

To study how the early believers related to the state, Romans 13:1–7 is a key, and sometimes controversial, passage to consider.

> Let every person be subject to the governing authorities; for there is no authority except from God, and those authorities that exist have been instituted by God. Therefore whoever resists authority resists what God has appointed, and those who resist will incur judgement. For rulers are not a terror to good conduct, but to bad. Do you wish to have no fear of the authority? Then do what is good, and you will receive its approval; for it is God's servant for your good. But if you do what is wrong, you should be afraid, for the authority does not bear the sword in vain! It is the servant of God to execute wrath on the wrongdoer. Therefore one must be subject, not only because of wrath but also because of conscience. For the same reason you also pay taxes, for the authorities are God's servants, busy with this very thing.

> Pay to all what is due to them—taxes to whom taxes are
> due, revenue to whom revenue is due, respect to whom
> respect is due, honour to whom honour is due.

For over fifteen hundred years, these verses have not troubled the Christian church too much. For most of European history, the church and the state have been in league with each other. To obey the state was to obey the church, and to obey the church was to obey God. However, things have been changing over the last two hundred years or so. Church-state links have been eroded in many countries (and dissolved in some), and are set to become even more tenuous. How, then, should we read these seven verses today?

As a minister I always feel uncomfortable when this passage is taken at face value and out of its immediate context. Some people want to accept the plain, simple reading of these verses. In congregations I have served in over the years, there have been those who believe we should just "do as we are told" as the people telling us are "in charge". Sometimes they have even added, "and they know best". These verses have also been used by tyrants over centuries as justification for terrible acts of injustice, exploitation and even genocide. In short, they have been used to validate empire. There have been rich and powerful people who have insisted that citizens should do as the state says. This is because it has been in their economic self-interest to do so. If people had started to rock the boat and challenge why things are as they are, they might well have lost their privileged position.

The experience of those who suffered at the hands of the Nazis in Europe during the Second World War caused many Christians to question whether our received understanding of Romans 13 was correct. It has been said that these seven verses have caused more unhappiness and misery in the world than any other group of verses from the New Testament, as tyrants have used them to justify some terrible atrocities.

One problem is that these verses seem so clear in what they are saying. They appear to be directive about behaviour: be subject, do not resist authority, do good, pay taxes and respect and honour those who deserve respect and honour. There are also warnings about judgment and vengeance for those who do not do what is expected.

Paul teaches something quite different in other parts of the New Testament. The apparent clarity of this passage makes it stick out like a sore thumb amongst his other writings. These seven verses do not even appear to fit very well into the two chapters of which they form the central part (Rom. 12–13).

Romans 13:1–7 also does not fit into our understanding of the Biblical story we have journeyed along so far in this book. For instance, on the basis of this text, the Children of Israel would not have resisted Pharaoh, and Moses would have passively given in to him. The great Exodus would never have happened. God's people would have remained in slavery and the Ten Commandments would not have been given at Sinai. Yet, interestingly, Paul appeals to the commandments in the verses that follow (Rom. 13:8–10).

Today, we live in quite different democratic societies that value human rights and encourage us to question the integrity and wisdom of those who rule us. Freedom of speech and an independent press have helped to uncover injustices approved by those in high office. We know rulers should always be held accountable by those they are elected to serve.

What shall we do then with this awkward set of verses in Romans 13? Here are some common approaches.

There are those who simply will not accept Paul wrote this. They say it is so out of harmony with his other teachings, let alone the witness of the rest of the Bible, it could not have come from his pen. It must have been inserted at a later stage by those in the empire who were attempting to impose control and authority on the church.

Then, there are some who say this passage makes sense in its political setting when there was an anti-Jewish climate in Rome. Jews had been made scapegoats and exiled from the city because of the riots and unrest that occurred during Nero's rule. Eventually, these Jews were guardedly allowed back into Rome where the Gentile Christians welcomed them into their congregations. They were, therefore, putting themselves in danger of angering the authorities. Paul effectively told the believers to "keep your heads down, obey the authorities and do not draw attention to yourselves". On this interpretation, the passage should not be applied universally. It was meant for a specific time and place.

My view is this: God intends there should be systems and institutions of government in order that we can enjoy the security of an ordered world and communities that nurture humanity. God does not ordain, though, any specific set of rulers; just the principle that there should be good government. From the early days of the church, Christians believed one must obey the state only in so far as it does not contradict the will of God, "We must obey God rather than any human authority" (Acts 5:29). If the state does not live up to its calling of being just and caring for all, then it must be challenged and called to account—but without violence. Paul does not want Christians to blindly accept all the state does, as if it is always correctly carrying out the will of God. Also he does not want them to rebel against it and tear apart the government that exists. There were some groups, such as the zealots, who were keen to instigate revolt, but Paul did not want the believers to have anything to do with them. He asserted that those who hold power have a part to play in what God wants for his world, but they need to play their part in a just and humane manner.

In the Old Testament, the Persian emperor Cyrus did this. He was called "anointed" as he led the exiles out of captivity back to Jerusalem (Isa. 45:1). He was never given any messianic status, he was simply an instrument unknowingly used by God. The same idea is present in Paul's thinking when he speaks of the governing authorities as "the servant of God" (Rom. 13:4). They are used by God, but they are unaware of it most of the time.

Paul had an extremely high respect for the rule of law. If he had done wrong, he agreed he should pay the price for it, even if it meant death (Acts 25:11). But if he had done no wrong (as he claimed when he was arrested, Acts 25:8) then he should be freed. He therefore instructed the believers to avoid doing anything that deserved punishment. They should seek to be obedient. As the passages surrounding Romans 13 affirm, they should bless those who persecute them (12:14), live in harmony with others (12:16), not strike back at those who do them evil (12:17), live peaceably with others as far as possible (12:18), and love their enemies (12:20–21). Love does not wrong a neighbour (13:10). Christians should live as honourable citizens (13:13). It is within this context Romans 13:1–7 must be read, with the caveat that the believers' first allegiance is to Jesus as Lord.

The church

The church was born at Pentecost with a variety of languages and, in time, across many of the cities of the Roman Empire, a network of assemblies and congregations developed which was marked by its diversity. When Archbishop Rowan Williams spoke about the need for the Church of England to become again a "mixed economy" church, he meant we should become much more open to variety and difference. This, he said, had deep theological roots, as there are mixed economy echoes in the Trinity: Father, Son and Holy Spirit have their own identities. They are distinct persons—but they are also totally involved with each other and mutually dependant on one another, so much so that they are a single entity. The seeds of this variety and mutuality were present at the birth of the church.

On the day of Pentecost, the church bore witness to the resurrection of Jesus, whom God raised from the dead. This was preached, in the main, to Jewish hearers. However, there were also many Romans on the sidelines who were aware that Peter and the apostles were announcing there was another king, other than Caesar. This king was the man the Romans thought they had finished with at his crucifixion—Jesus.

According to the book of Acts, each of the church congregations was a community of believers attempting to live out the gospel of Jesus in a manner that was both personal and public, private and political. These early Christian communities sought to take seriously the age-old story that started with Abraham, who left the gods of empire in order to follow the Lord, and the story of Moses, who led the people "out of the land of Egypt and out of the house of slavery". It is the way of life demonstrated in Jesus, in who he was, what he did and how he died at the hands of the Romans. In Acts, the baton of this alternative way of living was passed on to the network of churches. They were not the kingdom, but they were visual aids that could be pointed to when somebody asked, "What is the kingdom like?" These were subversive groups who refused to accommodate the cult of Caesar, because their allegiance was to Jesus. While living in this different way, they nonetheless sought to remain obedient citizens: paying taxes, obeying laws and seeking the common good. Spread throughout the empire, these cells were signs of God's other way, where the distinctions of race, gender and social class no longer determined a person's significance or power in the community. Even though there was great variety and diversity, everyone was one in the kingdom of Jesus (Gal. 3:28). Living this way, they were a light to the nations. They did what Israel failed to do (Isa. 42:6, 49:6).

Today, many people talk of becoming a Christian as if it is purely a personal spiritual experience. Paul was not offering this, nor would he have understood what it meant. To become a follower of Jesus was to sign up to the kingdom movement rooted in the radical agenda of the Ten Commandments. It was to enter a way of life, with an allegiance to Jesus as king that would be regarded as deeply counter-cultural. The gospel Paul preached was politically subversive: it had the potential to undermine the Roman way of doing things. N. T. Wright, a theologian and former Bishop of Durham, makes the point that Paul was not offering a new religious experience in his preaching. Rather, he was inviting people to sign up to become members of cells (churches) which were loyal to this new king Jesus and, by doing so, to follow God's alternative way of living.[3] This would be in contrast to the pattern of life on offer in the world around them. When Paul was eventually arrested for his work, he took his imprisonment and persecution as confirmation that he had done his job properly. This new way of living, this alternative to empire, was proclaimed as the first taste of the way things will eventually end up in God's new world order.

These new assemblies of believers were not just places for Sunday services and home Bible study groups; they were political as well as religious meeting places. They did not plan revolution or rebellion; they sought to live Jesus' alternative way while still within the empire. In doing this they had to negotiate how to live *in* the world while not being *of* it. The mission of the church was not simply to increase its numbers. That would be to follow the typical agenda of empire that wants to have more and be significant in the eyes of those who look on. The mission of the church was to announce that God is present in the world and calls people to live according to his way of doing things; a way opposed to domination, exploitation, and control over others. It was, therefore, incumbent upon these small Christian communities they should live lives that matched this message. The church in Acts followed the example of Jesus by including and embracing those who were marginalised by empire ways of living: women (especially widows), the poor, tax collectors, sinners and slaves.

Christ crucified

The gospel of Jesus was a threat to the powers-that-be and the status quo, but not by using the violent ways of empire, which is what the Roman authorities would have expected. The non-violent gospel the church proclaimed was rooted in the subversive actions of the crucified Christ. Paul continues his ministry in this vein. He was blatantly anti-Roman in his focus on the crucified Christ. He boldly declared, "We proclaim Christ crucified, a stumbling-block to Jews and foolishness to Gentiles" (1 Cor. 1:23). To say the one crucified by the Romans was now becoming the Lord of all was offensive to the Jewish constituency and laughable to the Romans. As I have already pointed out, experience on the street was that believers were sometimes accused of turning the Roman world upside down. In all of this, though, Paul asserted he was not against people or individuals, "For our struggle is not against enemies of blood and flesh" (Eph. 6:12). His struggle was against the spirit of empire: the way authorities operate, the values cultures adopt and the methods of imperial economics. He calls them rulers, authorities, cosmic powers and spiritual forces. In basic terms, Paul's message to the church and to the believers was, "Do not rebel and attack, but pray, resist and live the alternative way of Jesus."

Paul's message about the crucified Christ did not only have implications for how politics worked; it clearly had a political message at its very core. It was a new way of seeing every aspect and facet of life. It is to our shame that what started out as an anti-empire movement eventually became the official religion of the Roman Empire. This partnership ultimately proved to be toxic and violent.

Paul did not believe violence was Christ-like. He saw that the powers and authorities that adopted such an approach were doomed to destruction. The seeds of their own downfall were within them. All empires eventually fail. Colonies demand independence, corporations and large companies eventually overstretch themselves and go bankrupt, and cultural hegemonies become eclipsed by other movements. If we attack them brutally, we only serve to multiply the evil and adopt the very ways we claim to oppose. Paul did not seek to attack and destroy, but sought to know only Jesus, and him crucified (1 Cor. 2:2). Jesus' death on the cross was at the centre of God's plan for overthrowing the powers of the world. Jesus was not violent to others; instead he absorbed the world's violence in his own body. Through the cross, the empires were seen for what they were: bullying, exploitative, fearful and murderous. In their desperate attempt to hang on to power they made a spectacle of themselves by executing an innocent individual, the king of the true kingdom. It is amazing how destabilising an approach, such as Jesus', can be. Others have employed Jesus' tactics. Ghandi's simple non-violent gestures helped give energy to India's claim for independence from the British Empire. Martin Luther King's insistence on preaching resistance gave momentum to the American Civil Rights movement. This is the power of powerlessness.

The resurrection

In the resurrection of Jesus, the initial call and promise to Abraham was fulfilled. The alternative way of living that had always been intended for humanity was seen, demonstrated and vindicated in Jesus. He was a vivid intensification of all that was called for, given and commanded in the Old Testament. If you want to know how to fulfil the commandments of Sinai, then look at Jesus. His life was not an overwhelming demonstration of God's forceful power, but the power of suffering love. In the resurrection of Jesus, we have a breakthrough into the way of doing things that God had always wanted for the world. Something happened at the empty tomb that could not be reversed—just like when a baby is born, you cannot change your mind and go back to how it was before.

For Paul and all the early believers, the risen Jesus was their future. The poor and the outcasts were no longer outsiders; they had become insiders when Jesus himself became poor and outcast. They were no longer hopeless, as the defeated one had become the resurrected one. Peace was established, not in the Roman way of military conquest and the imposition of conformity, but through Jesus' self-giving. Those who invest in the way of empire will never understand this. To the Gentiles it was utter foolishness. To the Jews, who should have realised, it was a stumbling block. They just could not see it.

The book of Revelation

The final book of the Bible is loved by some, feared by others and misunderstood by most. However you read it, you cannot get away from its anti-imperial message. Here, Babylon is the archetypal empire. It stands for all empires that will eventually be overcome by the empire of God. At the time John wrote this book, Babylon stood for the Roman Empire.

John writes to relatively new churches that were very much aware of the domination of the empire. He called these Christian communities *Ekklesia*, which we translate into English as "church". His understanding of church was a far cry from our modern-day expressions. In Roman society, *Ekklesia* were the political assemblies that governed the cities, similar, in some ways, to our city councils. John called these young congregations by the same term. For him, the lives of the Christian *Ekklesia* were intended to be models of how God would have things be in a community that followed Jesus. If the *Ekklesia* of the Roman cities were an expression of empire, then the *Ekklesia* of the believers were to be examples of the kingdom of God.

While the culture and economy of empire were seductive and inhumane in nature, Rome did not impose emperor-worship on the people by force. However, it was not possible to participate socially and economically in society if one did not take part in the cult of Rome to some degree. As a result, it was all too easy to be drawn into the religion of Caesar and the ways of empire.

John, like Paul, did not call for revolt or violence against Rome, but his call was strong. First, his message was about the worship of God, not the emperor.

> To the one seated on the throne and to the Lamb be blessing and honour and glory and might for ever and ever! (Rev. 5:13)

Second, as Abraham was called out of the original Babylon, so too the people of the churches were called out of Rome, as it increasingly demanded their absolute loyalty.

> Come out of her, my people, so that you do not take part in her sins, and so that you do not share in her plagues. (Rev. 18:4)

As with the prophet Daniel centuries earlier, John believed they could only worship the "Lord God", not any god; they could only acknowledge the lordship of Jesus, not of Caesar. For John, Rome was no longer an empire they should do business with. It was not possible to negotiate a way of living within it. The Empire had instead, finally, become Satan incarnate.

John's hopeful imagination was expressed in a vision of God's reality. What he saw was not simply a restoration of the twelve tribes of Israel; it was more than this. His was a diverse and multi-cultural vision where no one race or idea was dominant over another (Rev. 7:9). This was no afterlife away in a distant heaven. John "saw" a new city "coming down from heaven" to the earth (Rev. 21:1,10). The home of God was to be among his people, his kingdom as heaven on earth.

John's style was apocalyptic, like Daniel's. His vision looked beyond the bounds of space and time for God to do something. He believed this had happened in Jesus Christ and would be completed at the end of time, when there would be a new heaven and earth.

The word "apocalypse" comes from a Greek word that means to uncover, or remove a veil. It was John's task to help believers in the *Ekklesia* see beyond their present situation to another reality—God's kingdom—even amidst persecution.

The book of Revelation is less about the end of the world and more about how to live in the present time. It is addressed to small communities of resistance that were trying to hold onto the memory of Jesus while being bombarded with the propaganda of *Pax Romana*. It took courage to believe something different to the dominant story.

In this book is the call to loyal endurance (Rev. 1:9, 13:10, 14:12). The people of the *Ekklesia* were to resist imperial threats and punishments. They were to be loyal in their worship to the Lamb on the throne. They were to be a people of hope.

Questions for discussion

1. Do you think we have tended to over-emphasise the personal spiritual experience of Pentecost and ignore the implications it has for the way we deal with our wealth?

2. What have you usually understood "conversion" to mean? In what ways was Paul's experience on the road to Damascus unsettling rather than comforting?

3. As Christians we have our identity in Christ, symbolised by baptism. How do we maintain this identity in a world committed to greed, control and the propaganda of empire that wants to take us into its way of life?

4. Paul announced Jesus was Lord and Saviour, not Caesar. Who or what do we rely on, in place of Jesus, to make our lives meaningful and whole?

5. How are we called to live death and resurrection daily in our lives?

Prayer

Lord Jesus Christ
who calls us,
not to comfort and consolation
    but to death
    and resurrection,
Teach us first to live
in the Spirit of Pentecost
    that you may
      set us alight with love
      to pledge our allegiance to you
      and serve our neighbours
on our street
and across the world.
Amen.

Notes

1. Luke Timothy Johnson, *Prophetic Jesus, Prophetic Church: The Challenge of Luke-Acts to Contemporary Christians* (Eedrmans, 2011), pp. 74–5.
2. Jonathan Sacks, *The Dignity of Difference: How to Avoid the Clash of Civilizations* (Continuum, 2002).
3. N. T. Wright, "Paul's Gospel and Caesar's Empire," in *Paul and Politics: Ekklesia, Israel, Imperium, Interpretation,* ed. Richard A. Horsley (Trinity Press, 2000), pp. 160–183; 161–2.

CHAPTER 10

Church and Empire

As recounted in the first few chapters of the book of Acts, the early church experienced two quite different phenomena: rapid growth and martyrdom. It is clear Luke saw both as a consequence of the coming of the Spirit. Today, when we talk of the work of the Spirit, we want to limit the conversation only to that which is positive and pleasing. When we ask the Spirit to move in our churches, we do not expect anyone might suffer for their faith or that the church's situation might start to feel more precarious—at least, not in the West. If our experience of life in the church is not about getting increasingly better and stronger, we tend to assume the Spirit of God is not with us. This, it could be argued, is another sign the spirit of empire is still very much with us in the church.

The experience of life for Christians in the first three centuries was particularly hard and difficult. They were oppressed and at times severely persecuted, being imprisoned, burnt alive and thrown before lions. These were undoubtedly distressing times for them, but they did not see it as evidence that God had abandoned them. Hope, though, is still hard to hold on to in the face of such violence and loss. The dominant religious cults of the Roman Empire were all around them with their attendant rituals. Some believers must have begun to wonder if the God they knew in Jesus Christ was up to the job.

Christendom

In AD 312, there was a momentous and unexpected development that affected everything: Constantine, the Roman Emperor, converted to Christianity. The Christians, who had previously been a persecuted minority, became the bearers of the faith for the empire. What had been the faith of the few became the imperial religion. This changed their fortunes completely.

As you can probably guess, tomes have been written on the reasons why Constantine made this dramatic change of allegiance. It may have been due to his belief that the Christian God was with him when he defeated a rival in war. It may have been because he believed Christ appeared to him in a dream. It may simply have been political expediency; that through co-opting the growing influence of the Christians, his power and position would be enhanced. However, establishing the truth of the matter is not our purpose here. The effect of this great upheaval is what is relevant to our study.

For most Christians, Constantine's conversion was accepted as good news, and I can understand why. If your sons had been thrown to the lions, your daughters raped, or your brothers burnt alive, you too would see this development in positive terms. The once beleaguered believers now had to try and understand what it meant to have the Emperor and the Empire on their side. The feelings of utter relief that they would no longer be attacked and vilified must have been palpable. It is no surprise that many regarded what happened as an act of God. Before their very eyes, they saw Rome (the kingdom of this world) become "the kingdom of our Lord and his Christ." This was seen as a massive victory for the gospel and a great success for the church. They trusted that the injustices and abuses of the pagan cults were to come to an end. It seemed the faith of the martyrs had been vindicated; they had not died in vain—but such an apparent victory did not come without cost.

Constantine worked to unite the Empire under the confession of the Nicene Creed. Here we see emerging two of the tendencies of empire: the co-option of religion to the imperial project and the imposition of uniformity by insisting everyone be held to the same doctrine. The establishment of the church as the central feature of empire is sometimes referred to as "Christendom". The term originated in the medieval period to describe the Christian world that developed. It appeared as if the church had taken the same wrong turning as Israel did in the Old Testament when it opted to have a king "like the other nations". The church was now a major player among the nations, and would be for centuries to come.

Christendom established itself in that part of the world where the power of the church prevailed—Europe. Christians had influence, political power and a good deal of wealth. In the thirteenth century, it is alleged Thomas Aquinas once called on the Pope when he was counting out a large sum of money: "You see, Thomas," said the Pope, "the church can no longer say, 'Silver and gold have I none.'" "True, Holy Father," was the reply; "and neither can she say, 'Rise up and walk.'" Because of all the riches the church now had, it assumed it was blessed by God, a mistake that King Solomon also made, and one that is still made today in some wealthier congregations.

Modernism to post-modernism

The power of Christendom waxed and waned over the centuries, but it increasingly lost its privileged position as two new movements eventually emerged in Europe: the Reformation of the sixteenth century and the later new cultural movement, the Enlightenment, of the seventeenth and eighteenth centuries. Before its power declined, Christendom was characterised by the dominant and often abusive power of the clergy, myth, superstition and irrationality. The Reformation sought to bring the church back to the faith of the Bible and to rid the church of the abuses of the clergy. It was the Bible, rather than the church, that was to become the authority in many churches across northern Europe. The Enlightenment movement believed in power and control through knowledge (scientific, political, economic and psychological). This became the new authority, which supplanted the authority of the church and the Bible in the public arena; an authority the church had enjoyed throughout the centuries of

Christendom. A new empire, built on rationalism and objectivity, was rising as the old one was eclipsed.

Today, we are now on the tail end of the wane of Christendom, so much so that we now say we live in a secular culture. If, therefore, this church-based imperial mind-set is no longer dominant, we must ask ourselves if this is a good thing. It seems to me there is something good in what is happening, even if we face a future of difficulty and decline in the church as, once again, we leave the privilege of empire for exile.

Those of us who are over 50 years old are, generally speaking, children of the Enlightenment. As such, we are modernists. This affects our thinking, our values and our choices more than we will ever realise. Many good things have happened as a result of its influence: scientific and technological progress, particularly in the richer nations, has led to dramatically improved health and longevity; education for all; raised living standards; increased trade; the creation of national and international infrastructures. There have been giant leaps forward in our understanding of the world and the universe, which have brought benefits to so many areas of life. We know so much more about our faith and its origins than ever before because of advances in archaeology, Biblical studies and linguistics.

However, not all of this "progress" has been good. It is rare a great gift does not also have its own great shadow. As a result of modernism, we now have more than enough nuclear weapons to destroy all the people on the planet. More is produced and consumed than the earth can sustain. The science that has brought us so much is now telling us the planet is becoming sick through pollution and climate change. Even though we possess more than we have ever had, we are no happier. We suffer more stress than ever before. An increasing number of commentators are telling us the Enlightenment worldview is running out of steam[1]. Yet another (cultural) empire is in decline.

For more than three hundred years, Western culture has been developing the modernist mind-set. It is still the same old story of domination and control, but in a different guise. It is a story we Christians have believed and trusted in, probably more than the mystery of the death and resurrection of Jesus Christ. As modernism also nears its end, we face a social and economic revolution, which may turn out to be bigger and far wider reaching than any of us can guess. It will, increasingly, feel as though we are entering liminal space, that place where we do not feel at home, having lost an apparently secure past without finding a new future. This is not only true for us as the church, but also for our culture, which may well make our experience of exile all more the deeper.

It seems too obvious to state that what follows modernism is post-modernism, but this is what the culture we are currently experiencing is sometimes. Today's younger people have a post-modern mind-set, which sees the world in completely different terms than those of us who are, on the whole, modernists. Post-modernism is not easy to pin down or define. It seems to be clearer about what it is not—modernism—than what it is. It is suspicious about authorities and institutions and any explanations or beliefs that claim to be valid for all religions, cultures, traditions, or races. It regards the relative truths of each person as sovereign. Concrete experience is important for the post-modern person, more so than principles, ideas and concepts. Attitudes are more important than facts. Post-modernism does not believe in universal truths or over-arching stories throughout history. Because there is no one single story that we are all a part of, everybody has to work out for themselves what the truth is and what the meaning of life is. In post-modernism, we each have to create our own reality; we are each very much on our own.

Post-modernism's basic criticism of modernism, however, should be taken seriously. It believes modernity is arrogant and smug in judging and dismissing other points of view, beliefs and convictions. Modernism stands condemned of building a new tower of Babel, this time by control through knowledge. Post-modernism claims all meta-narratives (over-arching stories) are suspect, as they are all power games. What is missing from both worldviews, of course, is the pre-eminence of love.

For many of us, post-modernity may well feel more like a place we are passing through, rather than a destination we have arrived at. In this sense, it is very liminal. In this no-where place we have some waiting to do. The temptation for many will be to go back to what we know—modernism. Just like the children of Israel who came out of Egypt, it is tempting to go back to what we know, even if it harmed us. An important work awaits us, however, which will not be possible if we revert back to our old certainties. The work we have to do is the slow work of waiting for the prophet's voice. We need to wait for what we do not yet possess, even though this is not an easy place to linger.

The call of God is for us to accept his other way, which rejects the tactics of power and domination and has its roots in the kingdom of God. The church must become its herald. For this, though, we need time and space. We need to become patient and realise what is to come does not depend on us, but on God. God has still got something to do and this is our hope. Waiting in liminal space is not an easy or pleasant task, but if we rush into action we are in danger of bouncing into something else as imprisoning as the past. This, then, is the work I believe the church must give itself to at this present time, and as we wait, we wait for the voice of God through prophets.

The sickness of anxiety

To make sure we do not move on too quickly to the next thing, we must consider three important tasks of our journey. Firstly, we must deal with our anxiety. We live in an anxious age and we belong to an anxious church. This anxiety is fuelled in the world by unrelenting economic uncertainty. The world we are losing has, for so long, been "normality" to us. The certainties and promises of Western progress no longer hold true, though, and we suspect our children and grandchildren may have a lower standard of living than us. This becomes a worry. We have lived with the assumption that a higher standard of living is always better and that it will always make us happier. It may turn out, of course, our children will be happier and more fulfilled with less.

We are also anxious about the church. Many church people, from a wide variety of traditions and denominations, say we must be involved in mission activity, otherwise "there will be nothing left of the church in a couple of generations." In their anxiety, they are consumed about the decline of the church, and their spur to action comes not from love, but fear. Most of us have not been taught how to hold our anxiety and so defuse it of its power. We immediately jump into action, any action, to make sure we are doing something to stem the decline. Even if we do not plough into activity, we will most likely come up with an explanation for why things are as they are. It hardly matters what the explanation is, as any will do. We seem to believe that by our actions and explanations we can keep our anxiety at bay—but it is not working. The radical theologian, Herbert McCabe, believes the root of all sin is fear. This explains why our anxiety takes us away from God's life, rather than deeper into it.[2] When we find ourselves in liminal space, we have to hold our anxiety and believe God is in the void; otherwise we become sick with fear.

The work of loss

Secondly, we need to work through our grief. We do not like losing, but we have all lost and will continue to lose. Loss is a part of life and we have to learn how to deal with it, even seeing how it can contribute to our growth as human beings. The Bible invites us to deal with our loss through weeping and mourning. It is an acceptance of how things are—the reality of our situation. Jesus said, "Blessed are those who mourn", but the world does not believe this or tolerate it. Yet it is only through weeping and mourning that a new future can emerge. This is how healing happens at a personal or community level. It is only when we feel and experience our grief that we can receive hope; the conviction that God has still got something to do. It is no surprise, therefore, that one third of the Psalms are about grief, mourning and weeping. These Psalms of lament are an important resource to us at times of loss.

We do not seem to want to mourn, though. It feels too much like failure and nothing at all like success—but in a culture that has lost its way and a church that has lost the privilege of Christendom, we must learn to weep. The trouble is mourning just does not seem very productive. It feels like a waste of time. We must learn from the exiles in Babylon who discovered the importance of weeping as they sat on the banks of the imperial river. Without weeping and mourning there is no healing. And if there is no healing, there is no newness. We must find the courage to admit our loss and embark on the journey of grief.

All those who work with people who are bereaved know mourning is essential and takes time. We have lost so much and there is probably further loss still to come. What is more important than saving the church as we know it is for the church to do her work of grief. Without this, our time in exile will be that much longer.

Prophetic imagination

Thirdly, we must be a people who look for prophetic imagination. Today, an increasing number of church leaders feel we need a new and fresh imagination in the church. This, though, is something more than the everyday imagination we might use when telling a child a bed-time story or when designing a piece of artwork. Prophetic imagination is a way of seeing an alternative future that can only be recognised by using a different mind-set. It is not the gift of strategising. It does not speak a plan into being; it is not technical or detailed. Instead, it uses open language that helps to reframe the big picture. Ultimately, newness does not come from human ingenuity, but as a gift from God. It is a gift that seems to be rare, not because God is reluctant to give, but because we are not ready or able to receive.

Prophetic imagination tends to emerge in liminal space: in moments of chaos, loss and change. It is hard for most of us to receive as we are usually caught up in our anxieties and fears; so consumed with our little worlds that we cannot see new possibilities. It is, however, in these times of deep crisis that a few people are able to help us do our hoping; they are the prophets among us. Just like in the Old Testament, they rarely come from the privileged elite or from centres of power, but from the edges of the community. They are able to see differently from this perspective. They tend to live slower, simpler lives. They are comfortable spending time in solitude and silence, as it is in contemplation and reflection that they are able to listen—to God and the world. They take Sabbath seriously. Often they will look like time-wasters, lazily wandering through life while the rest of us are busily trying to "keep the show on the road". In this slower life, though, they see what many of us would never see.

Church or kingdom agenda

Alan Roxburgh is a pastor, writer and consultant with more than 30 years' experience in church leadership and education. He says there is nothing more boring, unhelpful or further from God's imagination than the question, "How can we make the church work?" Many church leaders would respond loudly to Roxburgh's comment with "Here, here!" It feels like ministry has been reduced to the utilitarian and the pragmatic. Together with this, there is an assumption that churches with bigger congregations have got something right, while the smaller ones have not. Again, it is as if we have given in to the values of the gods of the empires around us, that more is better and powerful is good. We must learn that activism will not bring the newness we crave. Instead, we need to learn to live by another story, the ancient one that has its roots in Sinai and in the life and death of Jesus.

The uncertainty we face in the church today should not frighten us. Jesus was constantly leading his disciples across boundaries and into unknown territory. He took them to quiet places, up mountains, across the Sea of Galilee to be amongst pig farmers, and sent them out two by two with inadequate resources.

The church has a different agenda to worldly organisations. In time, nearly all organisations settle for the same agenda—that is, to continue to exist. I see this in schools, churches, advice centres, businesses and community associations. Initially, they may have a great passion for a certain purpose, but over time the need to survive takes over.

I am particularly struck by how this occurs in the military. The British Army claims it exists to defend the nation and serve its interests. Recently, our forces have been reducing in size. Some of the regiments and units have been merged or disbanded. As this happened, the cry went up, "Oh, but our regiment has a great tradition to which the people in our county have been so loyal over many years. It is like a family to us!" For these people who protest, the purpose of the army is no longer only about defending the nation; it has become increasingly about tradition, belonging and loyalty. As a result, they vigorously oppose their unit or regiment being disbanded. For them, it must continue to exist.

What I see happening in the army is so true of most organisations, including the church. We also so easily lose touch with the agenda of the kingdom of God. The church's purpose is to be the community that announces the reign of God as a radical alternative to the empires of the world. As William Temple, a former Archbishop of Canterbury, is once reputed to have said, "The church is the only institution that exists primarily for the benefit of those who are not its members." Many congregations, though, are sadly focussed on survival and growth.

The call to the kingdom of God is profoundly counter-cultural, and always has been. The economy, the markets and our consumerist culture do not tolerate such subversion easily. The empires have never been accommodating to the poor, the peacemakers, those who do not consume much, the humble, the persecuted or those who mourn.

It is ironic that the gospel has generally been proclaimed by those who are comfortable and powerful in the world's terms. This almost guarantees we will miss the point. It is not possible to preach a subversive gospel to the rich and powerful, while being rich and powerful. The troubles we now see coming to the Western church may well bring great blessings with them, as we start to see things from a position of disadvantage and less power. Being on the margins will not just change how we feel; it will also change what we believe.

The church, therefore, must recover its prophetic voice. It must tell the hopeful story of liberation in the face of empire. It must tell it more by its faithful witness than by its words, as the church is God's primary visual aid of kingdom living.

Questions for discussion

1. In what ways has the church historically followed the patterns of empire? How does it still do it today? Are there patterns of empire evident in your local church? Is the tendency to centralise church life evidence that empire is still alive and well among us?
2. What was good and what was bad for the church when Constantine converted to Christianity? What marks of Christendom do you see in: (a) our Western culture? (b) your church denomination or tradition?
3. Why are we so consumed with anxiety about the church and its apparent decline? How might we, as the church, begin to grieve about what we have lost? What do you understand "prophetic imagination" to mean? How have we followed a "church" rather than a "kingdom" agenda?

Prayer

O Spirit of God,
    present at creation
    and the birth of the church,
heal us
    of our sickness of anxiety.
In a world that wants more,
    help us to be
    content with enough,
    and to learn that in this
    we can find happiness.
Grant us fresh imagination
    in order that we might see your future,
    and not be blinded
    by our own preferences,
    wants and desires.

In the name of the King who is free,
Jesus Christ.
Amen.

Notes

1. Theologian Langdon Gilkey argues that the overriding spiritual and cultural fact of our generation is the end of the Enlightenment. He claims it has not fulfilled its promise to control the natural forces that threaten human life, reduce poverty through economic abundance or eradicate religious superstition by establishing rational and moral political structures. See Kyle A. Pasewark and Jeff B. Pool (Eds.), *The Theology of Langdon B. Gilkey: Systematic and Critical Studies* (Mercer Univeresity Press, 2000).

2. For a comparison of the different ways anxiety and love work see: Mark Yaconelli, *Contemplative Youth Ministry: Practising the Presence of Jesus with Young People* (SPCK, 2006), p. 51.

CHAPTER 11

Hope Beyond Empire

The story of the Bible starts and finishes with the call of God (Gen. 12:1, Rev. 18:4). This call is to leave the usual way of the world and journey in God's way of freedom, transformation and humility—but this does not come easily to us. Nations want to be great, churches also want to be great, organisations want to be impressive and individuals want to be regarded highly in the eyes of their peers. We want our country to keep up with other successful nations or, better, keep ahead of them. We want our church congregations to be big and lively, like the one down the road; we want to make a name for ourselves. This impulse, the Bible tells us, is not of God. It is part of the fatal flaw which has crept into the ways things are.

As individuals, we have been seduced. The urge to give in to the ego has overcome us. We have made choices that have led us along the wrong path. This has caused us, and others around us, much suffering.

It is not only individuals, though, who have sold out to egotism. States, authorities, companies and other organisational structures have a form of this—a collective egotism. This manifests all the traits of personal egotism: the need to be significant, better, more successful and powerful than others. This inevitably leads to conflict and anguish. This is the story-line of empires throughout history and, indeed, the story-line of history itself. The sickness that lies at the heart of each person also infects our institutions, communities, organisations and businesses. Once this disease has infected our ways of working, it is hard to stop the rot.

The Bible calls the drive to promote our self-interest at the expense of others sin. Sin is not just about doing bad things; it is also about having a wrong orientation. It is a condition, not only a set of wrong actions. Once in this condition we cannot help but do bad things, as Paul himself knew so well (Rom. 7:14–25). Where do we go from here?

In answering this question, we normally jump too quickly to action. We ask, "What should we now do?" We somehow feel if we can manage the problem then we will solve it; if we get all the bits in the order, then we will find our way through.

At times, our desire to sort things out is just too wilful and functional, like the mechanic who said, "We took the motorbike completely apart, but we could not find the speed anywhere." Life and love are not so easily diagnosed or manipulated.

In an epidemic of activism we move too quickly to attack the problem and miss the only thing necessary. What we are earnestly searching for cannot be seen with the eyes of the spirit of empire; we have to have a different way of seeing. This other way of looking is called the contemplative way; the way offered to God's people throughout the story of the Bible. It is the alternative to the way of empire; in fact, it subverts the way of empire. It starts with silence, not violence. The world needs our silence. When we slow down and take time, we see things with greater clarity. This stance lies at the very heart of the Christian tradition, but is something we have lost. We have let the principle of Sabbath slip from our lives. The fruit of this has been bitter, allowing the spirit of empire to remain established in the world and deep in our lives.

A new way of being

Our first step is contemplation. The radical priest and peace activist, Daniel Berrigan, believes the practice of contemplation and how we deal with the powers-that-be go hand in hand. He has said that we need to regard contemplation as a strictly subversive activity, because it is rooted in the prophetic tradition of the Bible.

Unfortunately, meditation and contemplation have become big business—fashionable and profitable. Typing "meditation centre" into the Google search engine retrieves over 800,000 results. People are taking time out to try to help cope with our violent and stressful world. Retreat centres of all kinds have sprung up offering us quietness and restful respite. They help put distance between us and the terrible horrors of the world. They are literally an escape. If they only do this, then they are a danger, as they help us to become neutral and passive in a world which desperately needs our help. So many schools of contemplation and meditation, and the resources they produce, are concerned with avoiding conflict and reducing tension and anxiety, but not dealing with issues of justice. This emphasis has even become popular in our churches where spirituality has been reduced to an attitude we withdraw into to help us stop feeling the pain of the world. This is bogus contemplation.

By taking such retreats and practising their contemplation we become uncoupled from the real affairs of life and the world's suffering. As we become neutral and passive, we are recruited as a resource in support of the dominant culture; we are no longer people who resist it. We are placed out of harm's way, pacifying our anger, which should really be put in service against the spirit of empire. This passive contemplation has become a terrible drug; it has become a coping strategy for many. This sort of religion can be rightly accused of being "an opium of the people".

It is frightening how easy it has been for the dominant consumer culture to turn contemplation into a commodity, co-opting it to its cause. This is what empires do. "Spirituality" can now be bought and sold in many forms without it ever truly changing us or challenging the way things are in the world. Such spiritualities are not neutral, as they support oppressive and exploitative practices. They cry "Peace, peace" when there is no peace. In this bogus contemplation, we collude with evil rather than oppose it.

Faith is often about question and struggle before it is about certainty, comfort and peace. This was Jesus' experience at the start of his ministry. His forty-day "retreat" in the desert was no quiet break from life back in Nazareth. He struggled and fought in the desert place where there were no people. To put it bluntly, he had to decide if his ministry was to be rooted in the spirit of empire or the kingdom of God.

When we contemplate properly, we may encounter more strife than quietness. Some say contemplation should come with a health warning! More often than not, it is only in the silence that this conflict starts to emerge, where we begin to realise what is true and what is false, what is egotism and what is Spirit. It is only in solitude that we become fully awake.

As we consider towards the end of this book where we go from here, we must make sure we begin with a contemplative mind. This approach, this prayer, is not to be seen as an escape from the world, but as a way of sharing in the redemption of the world.[1] The aim of Christian contemplation is not inner peace, but the kingdom of God, in the individual and in society at large.

If we are to be people who can see beyond the world of empires, we need to be people of hope. This hope is found in God, and God is first encountered in silence.

New ways of relating

If the first step is contemplation, then the second step is to reassess the way we relate to one another and work together. In the kingdom of God, how things are done is even more important than what is done. Empires are the opposite; they are interested in what is done and pay less attention to how it is achieved. To find a new way of relating, we have to be clear about our starting point. At present, we are in a mess; we carry a lot of cultural baggage.

The story of Christendom has largely been a story about command and control rather than contemplation. The church has enjoyed a privileged and wealthy position as one of the main power brokers (sometimes the only power broker) in European societies. But as Christendom has been in collapse for some time now, the church no longer commands the respect and attention it once did. What was all very comfortable and self-serving is now exposed as institutionalised, self-absorbed and unsustainable. As we enter our own exile, we are now heading for something much less certain and more uncomfortable, which threatens our established way of doing things. The heydays of full churches, secure finances and strong influence within the nation are over. In this crisis, there is a strong urge to return to what we once had. We start to talk about survival, saying, "If we do not do something soon, there will be nothing left." We sound like people in the Old Testament after the fall of Jerusalem trying to recover what they have lost. We should not be concerned about our survival; just that we become the people we are meant to be.

If the end of Christendom feels bad enough, then the decline of modernism will make it feel all the worse as it invested everything in command and control. It became over-dependant on the belief that we could understand how the universe works and, therefore, master it. As our confidence in this story grew, so did our optimism and delusions of utopian grandeur. We thought we could finally fix the world and become masters of our own destiny. This myth of progress has been the driving force behind Western development. The belief in ever-increasing wealth and technological control has fuelled our economies and determined our values. Not only was this storyline applied to science and technology, but also to the way society functioned with its necessary institutions and organisations. We even invented a discipline called social science. We believed everything could be ordered to build ourselves a secure and certain future; another manifestation of the spirit of empire. This myth asserts that the whole of life could be treated as if it were a machine: taken apart, fixed and put back together again. This myth has deluded us into thinking we are in control.

This story has also run out of steam. Our institutions, based on this worldview, are increasingly dysfunctional. Politicians are unable to do much economically coherent because the growth model we are following is broken, but politically they cannot say so. National governments find it difficult to work together to address climate change, financial regulation or other major crises, because they do not have a clear mandate or the power to impose the necessary solutions. Empire is failing and power structures are failing, as they always have.

We need a new story: a story which prioritises relationships between people over managing resources and processes. We need to rediscover the call of Abraham, the principles of Sinai and Jesus' kingdom of God. We need to find ways of being that generate new life and fresh creativity. The old Enlightenment story produced efficiency and wealth (for some), but in following this narrative we have polluted our souls as well as the planet.

Margaret Wheatley researches and writes about radically new practices and ideas for organising in chaotic times. She says we should look to the natural world for clues as to how life generates life. In nature, connection is important, as are autonomy and creativity. Nature harbours variety and diversity. Life does not arise from hierarchies but from connection and interaction. In fact, life has to link with other forms of life to prosper.

> Everywhere life displays itself as complex, tangled, messy webs of relationships. From these relationships, life creates systems that offer greater stability and support than life lived alone.[2]

We have grown up with the idea that resistance to change is a fact of life, but what life really resists is control. Any gardener knows this: when they go away for a couple of weeks over the summer they return to overgrown flower beds and rampant weeds in the lawn. We know this too in the workplace. If we box people in with too much restraint and over-bearing regulations, they usually start to resist and even fight back. If we isolate people, they look to build relationships in any way they can. We see this between prisoners kept in long-term isolation and enforced silence. They communicate by tapping softly on pipes or quietly whispering, no matter what the danger. Ultimately, it is impossible to impose control on anyone forever, since as humans we are designed to create life and connection.

This is the life God intended outside of Babylon, beyond Babel and in the wake of Pentecost. It is an energy that does not start with an imposed structure, plan or design, but with life itself. It comes from the interactions between people and communities who decide to come together. The gospel of Jesus is so much more about community than organisation. How things are done takes priority over what is done. The twelve tribes of Israel, before they chose to have a king at the top of a royal hierarchical structure, lived in a confederation, not a command and control system. They had to learn to negotiate their relationships and their differences and see how these could be configured to enhance life. Sadly, we tend to think people who do not "fit in" need a more controlling style of leadership. The prophets were people who refused to fit in, and God's people often killed them.

In Macclesfield, we had a family of four churches. Initially, they were set up with a hierarchical structure, a team parish, with me as team rector at the top. There were the usual groans and complaints that arise in such structures. Individuals and congregations accused committees and individuals further up the chain of command of getting things wrong, which made life difficult for them.

In 2010 we dismantled this structure and set up a completely different legal arrangement between the churches. In future, there would be no one committee or person that controlled everything. We decided we would negotiate what we would do together and what we would do apart. An important part of the clergy's role would be to stimulate and encourage collaboration and cooperation between the churches. The only overarching principle we retained was that we would pay the money due to the diocese together, and so continue to support each other, especially our smallest and poorest church. Some people thought we would lose our unity.

Following this change, however, the moaning and complaining across the team of four churches almost completely stopped and we did far more together than ever before. I, and the other clergy, had to learn to lead differently. We had to learn to trust people's humanness, which brought us some headaches, but mainly pleasant surprises. When we trusted people, they trusted each other. They became more curious about their differences, rather than more fearful. Our churches became quite optimistic (or rather, hopeful!) about what we could and should do.

The believers of the early church did not ignore structure. On the day of Pentecost, some sort of organising would have been needed as they shared their wealth with those in need. The Apostles were an organised leadership and soon deacons were appointed to make sure those in need were not overlooked as the church grew. They were light on structure, though; they did not make organising and running the church their highest priority. How they did things was more important than what they did. It did not mean they were free of problems, but despite these, the spread of the good news about God's way of doing things was significant.

Women and equality

In moving to find new ways of relating, we must address the most fundamental relationship of humankind—that between men and women. Here in Britain, one of the greatest social developments of the last century has been the place of women in society. Electoral reform granted women the vote (albeit in stages). Social reform improved their standing in law, reducing discrimination and affording them greater equality in employment, education and property rights. Sexual reform came as a result of effective contraception (particularly the wide availability of the pill) and the family planning movement. These reforms have given women increased freedom and power.

Despite all that has been achieved, there is still much to do though. Women are very much under-represented in significant leadership posts (e.g. in Parliament, the police force and in business). Their pay is generally 20 per cent lower than men's. More than one in four women report having experienced domestic violence during their lifetime and on average, two women are killed each week by a current or former partner. Women are often portrayed in the media in passive or sexualised roles.[3]

In other parts of the world, the situation is much worse. Women are abused and ill-treated in these places on such a wide scale that the reported number of victims is completely unbelievable. We need to get away from our egotistical positions on the roles of men and women, as there is so much more at stake—people's well-being and survival.

The church, as an institution, has not been at the forefront of campaigns for gender equality, even though 30 per cent of feminists would describe themselves as religious or spiritual, with a significant number being Christians. The reluctance of a mainly male-led, hierarchical church to deal with these issues confirms many people's impression about organised religion. As the feminist and trade union activist Cath Elliott wrote:

> Christianity is and always has been antithetical to women's freedom and equality, but it's certainly not alone in this. Whether it's one of the world's major faiths or an off-the-wall cult, religion means one thing and one thing only for those women unfortunate enough to get caught up

in it: oppression. It's the patriarchy made manifest, male-dominated, set up by men to protect and perpetuate their power.[4]

One of our difficulties is that the story of the Bible is highly patriarchal. In the Old Testament, this resulted in societies where women had few, if any, rights and so were treated as disposable. It was men who held all the power, property and freedoms. The temptation for men to dominate over women throughout history has been the same as the temptation for all humanity to follow the ways of empire. This is a world where those who have most brute strength usually win. Yet the Biblical story is rooted in the amazing declaration in the first creation account.

> God created humankind in God's image, in the image of God, God created them; male and female God created them. (Gen. 1:27, *author's adaption*)

This statement does not affirm in any way the domination of men over women. It does not even affirm that women and men are separately or individually made in the image of God. It is only together in unity, as the persons of the Godhead are together in unity, that humanity as male and female reflects the image of God. In God there is both female and male. There can be no separation, no domination, and no privilege amongst humans; there has to be equal participation, collaboration and trust.

Patriarchy is not God's idea. It is as alien to God as the ways of empire are. We know this because Jesus behaved as if the above statement about the creation of humankind was true. In the cruel patriarchal society of his day, Jesus treated women in the same way he treated men.

The witness of history shows us we have moved back to patriarchy from Jesus' way of relating to women just as we have moved repeatedly back to empire. Women have been robbed of the freedom Jesus gave them. We men have not had the courage to believe that God's ways will be better than the way of command and control. Until recently, there were very few female theologians. (The Church of England has only recently started to ordain women as bishops.) This has influenced our interpretation and understanding of scripture.

When Mary realised how special it was to be the mother of the Son of God, she sang an old song that included the revolutionary words:

> He has brought down the powerful from their thrones,
> and lifted up the lowly. (Luke 1:52)

We have not been very good at working with God to bring rulers down from thrones through subversive action or by lifting up the lowly. Our love of imperial ways has left us with too many powerful people on thrones of different sorts. On the matter of lifting up the lowly, I have been guilty as a preacher of asking people to forgive those who have sinned against them without also being attentive to the sin that had been committed against them in the first place. I have called for forgiveness without justice. Lifting up the lowly is more than caring for the needy. It is about ordering life in such a way that everybody can enjoy their basic rights as human beings. Many people need justice, not just forgiveness.

The Apostle Paul also quoted the words of a song. Talking of Jesus, it says:

> [He] emptied himself,
> taking the form of a slave,
> being born in human likeness. (Phil. 2:7)

As preachers we often encourage our congregations to become humble and empty when speaking from this text. This is good if we are speaking to people who are proud and full to any extent. There are many people, though, who have been seriously humiliated by the violent abuse of others. There are those who have suffered in the modern version of the slave trade, been trafficked or forced to work in the sex industry. They do not need to be asked to empty themselves; someone has already emptied them out. They need to be affirmed, empowered and lifted up.

Sadly, even more women are in this situation than men. We have to be careful how we use these texts. All of us who preach, lead, or are pastors in churches, need to become aware of the positions we preach from. None of us is totally objective. We all have a point of view—that is, we each view things from a single point. This is why we need to hear the voices of many people in the church, especially women, like Mary, who see the world from a lowly point.

Because we have not embraced all women have to offer, humanity has been travelling through life with a limp. Women have suffered, but so have men, if only they knew it. Together we reflect the image and glory of God and so together we will be able to see new possibilities for a new future. We are not going to be able to do it apart from one another.

Organisational models

To relate differently we need alternative ways of organising that will support relationships between people and build trust and cooperation. At the moment, the economies of the West, and increasingly other parts of the world, are dominated by the "investor ownership" model. In this model, investors are the only owners; other interested parties (employees, customers and local communities) are excluded. Such organisations and companies do not trade for the public good, but only to make profits for the owners. In fact, under British law the company directors owe no duties to anyone else.[5] Their responsibility is to maximise value for the shareholders; this is especially so in a public limited company (plc). Profits are usually withdrawn from the neighbourhood in which they were generated to increase the wealth of those who have little or no connection with that community. The quest of this model is continual growth and private gain. Henry Wallich, economist and former governor of the US Federal Reserve, said that so long as there is growth there is hope.[6] Unfortunately, this way of organising things has become such a dominant model that many feel this is the only way of doing business, even though it divides people rather than builds bridges between them. The aggressive competition we now have in the marketplace is the opposite of collaboration and cooperation.

There is reason to hope though. The economic collapse of 2008 has helped some people realise that this way of doing business is seriously flawed and there must a better way. In 2013, students at Manchester

University formed the Post-Crash Economics Society. They said nobody was explaining to them why the financial crash had happened and they were still being taught neoclassical economics as if it was the only theory. They felt their economics department was simply ignoring the reasons for the financial collapse. One online comment said, "We still just seem to have roughly seven fat years and seven lean years. We've known that since year dot. I don't think 'Economics' has got us much further."

The other significant model of recent history has been state ownership. Nationalisation has been generally discredited. Our experience of it has been that it leads to increasing inefficiency and bureaucracy. It has resulted in a mind-set of entitlement and expectation made worse by our ever increasing, dominant consumer culture. On top of this, we have seen too many examples of state ownership that themselves have become manifestations of the spirit of empire, here and abroad.

There are, however, alternative ways of doing business which are not designed around economic gain for just a few, but on self-help. These have their origins in the late eighteenth and early nineteenth centuries. They are the mutual organisations; sometimes wonderfully entitled "friendly societies" and also known as "building societies". They are rooted in people's need to organise themselves for their own common good. Initially set up to help address deprivation, these businesses are owned by the people who use them, whether they are customers, employees or residents, who themselves form their membership. Each member has an equal vote so nobody is excluded from the opportunity to shape any decisions that are made. When a surplus is made, it is distributed amongst the members and therefore retained in the community.

Today, there is renewed interest in mutual organisations among local communities as well as with an increasing number of politicians. The recent growth of the Credit Union Movement in Britain is a good example. These are financial cooperatives which provide their members with flexible savings and loans, again owned by the members. They are promoted by the churches, among other bodies, as ethical alternatives to high-interest loan companies.

In our own country, mutual organisations are owned by over 13 million people. Across the world, mutual organisations are a force for good, employing 100 million people with almost one billion members. They are a fascinating alternative to the imperial way of doing things.[7]

Unfortunately, many building societies, as mutual organisations, were privatised in the 1990s and became limited companies, proving that is all too easy in our economy for shareholders to take control and have priority over other stakeholders.

Mutuals are only one approach of doing business, and even within these there is a wide range of models and developments. There are also "not-for-profit" organisations and a whole assortment of community-owned and controlled enterprises, which help local neighbourhoods become increasingly self-reliant and sustainable. Operating under titles such as community enterprises, social enterprises and community businesses, they improve the quality of life for people through economic regeneration and social activity. These are all alternatives to the traditional and dominant investor-owner model, which inevitably tend towards an imperial way of working once the business turnover gets beyond a certain size.

The open source model of organising business and activity is an interesting and more recent development. It is a way of thinking and working which enables people to further their own interests while also contributing those interests back to a common good. This has been particularly popular in the development of computer software. Individuals are able to contribute to a project and receive from it without having to make or receive payments.

If you are aware of the open source way of working, it is probably because of some of the programs you use on your computer. The Mozilla Foundation, which produces the free web-browser Firefox, is one such organisation.[8] This is how it describes itself on its website:

> The Mozilla project is a global community of people who believe that openness, innovation, and opportunity are key to the continued health of the Internet. We have worked together since 1998 to ensure that the Internet is developed in a way that benefits everyone. We are best known for creating the Mozilla Firefox web browser.
>
> The Mozilla project uses a community-based approach to create world-class open source software and to develop

new types of collaborative activities. We create communities of people involved in making the Internet experience better for all of us.

As a result of these efforts, we have distilled a set of principles that we believe are critical for the Internet to continue to benefit the public good as well as commercial aspects of life.

There are many open source software projects, so much so that it is possible to carry out almost any task on a personal computer nowadays without having to buy any software applications from the large corporations.[9] These open source foundations call themselves communities in a broad and non-geographical sense. They are made up of people who have a common interest, who are willing to give as well as receive, and are open to working in relationships of trust. They also often state in their core values that a balance between commercial goals and public benefit is central to what they are doing.

The open source model has also been applied to the production of computer hardware as well as community organising and political activity. It prioritises transparency, collaboration, sharing and continual improvement. Open source working is valued not only for its improved ethic over the investor-owner model, but because it offers better quality, higher reliability and more flexibility at lower costs. It also spells the end to "customer lock-in", which makes a customer dependant on a company for its products or services and unable to use another product without substantial switching costs (Microsoft Windows is a prime example).

On the high street there are also signs of hope. Customers are now lobbying the large retailers to sell ethically sourced products. There are now Fairtrade approved products in most of the large supermarkets.[10] Communities are organising themselves so their village, town, city or borough achieves Fairtrade status. Small retailers are fighting back against the dominance of the supermarkets. In the village of Tideswell, Derbyshire, local shop-keepers have set up their own online shop. They do not want to see the decline of their high street, so local people can now buy groceries via their website and have them delivered to their door.[11] As far as possible, everything they sell is locally sourced, and they plan to add other goods and services in time.

These are all hopeful signs that the exploitative way of empire does not have complete dominance. They are all alternative ways of organising things, working together and doing business. In each of these there is, I believe, something of the kingdom of God.

Consumption

The energy that feeds today's investor-owner corporations comes from our consumerist culture. The West has now moved from the Enlightenment value of progress to the post-modern value of choice. The world is organised around the illusion of giving us all what we want through the provision of products, services, experiences, relationships or religion. In reality, the large financial conglomerates remain sovereign but trick us into believing they serve us by producing what we think we need.

If the motto of the Enlightenment was Descartes', "I think, therefore, I am", then the motto of our consumerist culture must be, "I spend, therefore, I am." Behind the drive to consume is the need to maintain or raise our standard of living in comparison with other people. One lady I knew in Birmingham summed up a key doctrine of consumerism when she said, "You never go backwards with what you have; you always have to go forward." If we do not raise our standard of living, we believe we will get left behind, look out of date, and be pitied by those who have better things than us. We are then forever on a treadmill, as there is always somebody else who has better possessions than us, making us feel inferior.

In 1986, the opening of a McDonald's outlet in Rome led to the creation of the Slow Food Movement, which subsequently evolved into the wider Slow Movement, advocating Slow Living, Slow Money, Slow Parenting, along with many other streams, including Slow Church.[12] The heart of the movement questions the unbridled materialism that fuels our global economy.

As Christians we are caught up in this madness as much as the next person. We read our Bibles claiming we do not have enough money and spend what money we have with little reference to Jesus and the Gospels. The story of the Bible starts in Genesis with what can be viewed as a song of praise to God for his generosity and provision in the seven days of creation. In the psalms that follow later, it is a celebration of abundance and the utter reliability of the fruitfulness of the earth. The story of Pharaoh, and other kings and emperors, though, tells us something different. "There is not enough!" they say, "Get more, get as much as you can, because there is not enough to go round." We are people who have been nurtured by the fearful spirit of Egypt, despite God's assurances. We take all we can afford, all we can get. Under the imperial way of doing things, the rich become richer and fewer, and the poor become poorer and more numerous.[13]

In his humorous (and slightly irreverent) book *How to be Idle*, Tom Hodgkinson asks if we could be happy to live with less.[14] If we needed fewer things, then we would not have to work such long hours to earn so much money to pay for them. The result would be that we would have more time to enjoy life. This disease of wanting more is nothing new though. Around the year AD 1300, the German theologian and mystic, Meister Eckhart, put it this way: "Spirituality has much more to do with subtraction than addition." We simply need to learn to live with less, desire less and find contentment with what we already have.

In 2010, Jose Mujica became president of Uruguay. He was hailed as being the world's poorest president. He chose not to take up the official luxurious residence the state provided for its leaders; instead, he opted to stay on his wife's ramshackle farm outside the capital just off a dusty track where they grew flowers as a small family business. He drove an old VW Beetle and gave away 90 per cent of his salary. This is a stark contrast to other world leaders' lifestyle and our own.

Globalisation

If it is consumption that feeds the dominant institutions and financial interests of Western societies, then it is globalisation that serves to make them even more efficient in gathering wealth to a few.

Globalisation is the process of increasing the interconnectedness of people, cultures and economic systems across the world. A good number of people have benefitted economically from this, including many who read this book—but many have not. The benefits of globalisation have generally gone to those who already have more than their fair share of the wealth in the world; many of the poorest have ended up even poorer. Agencies, such as Christian Aid and CAFOD, are not keen to debate whether they are pro- or anti-globalisation. For them, the important question is how international trade and business can be made to work most effectively for the poor. Many Christian agencies see the Sabbath principles I discussed in Chapter 4 (based on the cancellation of debts, equity and the redistribution of wealth) as the "missing link" between globalisation and poverty reduction.

Imperial ways of working have benefitted greatly from globalisation. The large corporate institutions and companies have been able to influence policy and exploit global networks. They have invaded most regions of the world, recreating themselves in their own image. The upshot of this is that globalisation is frequently linked to increasing inequality. The World Bank and the International Monetary Fund (IMF) are often accused of forcing Western economic models on nations that have quite different ways of doing business.

In 1991, India devalued the rupee in order to stimulate exports. Farmers were advised to grow commercial cash crops, like cotton and sugar, instead of staple food crops. To fund this change, the farmers had to go to the now privatised banks for loan finance. In time, the interest rate went up, the farmers defaulted on their repayments and many lost their small holdings (the story of the Rich Young Man we considered in Chapter 8 is as applicable today as it was then). Because food crops were no longer being grown in India, there was a famine. Christian Aid reported that the liberalisation of the market had crushed poultry production in Malawi and reduced the number of people employed in

Ghana's manufacturing sector by two thirds.[15] It led to a decrease of sugar cane production in Jamaica with a resultant rise in unemployment, drug dealing and prostitution.[16]

Duncan Green, of Oxfam, and Claire Melamed, of the Overseas Development Institute, point out that policies that make all nations do things similarly cause poverty. They say diversity is imperative:

> New research also points to the importance of national differences. The same policy reforms have different outcomes in different countries, depending on the structure of the economy, the initial distribution of assets, and the nature of economic and political institutions. . . . Even though the evidence points to the importance of diversity, developing country governments are pushed by international rule-making . . . towards greater homogeneity of policy response.[17]

They believe it is crucial to establish policies which make room for diversity rather than reduce it. This is what the story of Babel teaches us. God's way is not to make everyone do the same thing, speak the same language or follow the same economic policy. Diversity is one of God's gifts to his creation.

The environment

Along with the poor of the world, the great loser in the marriage between consumerism and globalisation is the environment. The present threat to our global environment is, of course, a threat to all of us. It is greater than any other challenge we face today, be that terrorism, economic collapse or nuclear fallout. Most of us feel overwhelmed by the enormity of the problem and we try to "do our bit" to help. The list of symptoms of this crisis is frightening: global warming, water shortages, food crises, pandemics, overpopulation, conflict over resources, rainforest and biodiversity depletion, overfishing and unpredictable weather patterns. People who propose solutions to these problems often use the buzz words "renewable" and "sustainability". One comment on the Internet said in a book review, "The more one tries to understand and to make sense of this crisis, the more overwhelmed, powerless, and disheartened one becomes."[18]

Lester R. Brown, president of the Earth Policy Institute, says there are four things we must do: cut net carbon dioxide emissions, stabilise the world's population, eradicate poverty, and restore the earth's eco-systems. In his book, *World on the Edge,* he outlines his plan to do this.[19] His concern, though, is for more than practical action. He says we not only need to save civilisation; we need to learn to become civilised.

We will all be affected by global warming, but the poor will be affected the most. Bangladesh and Ethiopia are in the worst possible position. A rise of one metre in sea level could permanently flood 21 per cent of Bangladesh (most of it being its best land) and displace more than 15 million people. The rising sea surface temperatures in the Indian Ocean have been blamed in part for the droughts that Ethiopia has suffered since 1996, and up to 10 million people are still at serious risk. Numerous examples can be cited. In 2009, the House of Bishops of the Church of England said, "Abandoning the poor to struggle with the consequences of climate change is morally unacceptable."

We have to say, though, that this has been very confusing for many of us. What, a few decades ago, seemed good for us—continual economic growth—is now viewed as bad for us. We are being asked to change our priorities and the way we live; to own up and admit to our addictive patterns of consumption that are destructive for everyone. This suicidal consumption is sometimes called ecocide.

What part does our faith have to play in all this? Our relationship with the rest of creation is intimately tied up with our relationship with God. We cannot say we love God and not love all he has made. God's commitment to us was not to save people from the world, but to save the world *with* its people. Living in a way which honours the planet, rather than threatens it, is living out what it means to be made in the image of God—for that is how God treats the world, by honouring it. When we do not honour creation, one of the first casualties is the human soul: we damage our own spirits. The life of the individual is intimately tied up with the life of the world.

The church must realise its mission is inextricably linked with the entire planet and the health of its environment, as well as with its people. We have in our story a message that is about not exploiting and dominating. It is a message which believes there is enough for everybody, because God is the great provider. In 1996, the churches in England endorsed the Five Marks of Mission.[20] The fifth one states that the mission of the church is "To safeguard the integrity of creation, and sustain and renew the life of the earth." This is not an optional add-on to our mission; it is a core part of it.

In 2007, the Environment Agency carried out a survey among leading environmentalists and scientists and asked them to name fifty things that will save the planet. Top of the list was to use less power, much less power, a lot less power. The next was surprising. It was that religious leaders needed to make the planet their priority. Tireless advocate for the environment, Nick Reeves, said, "The world's faith groups have been silent for too long on the environment. It is time they fulfilled their rightful collective role in reminding us we have a duty to restore and maintain the ecological balance of the planet." Fellow panel member, Paul Brown, argued that Christians and members of other faiths "already believe that it is morally wrong to damage the environment. The problem is that many people simply choose to ignore this."[21] They call us to motivate and organise our congregations, to act and make it an utmost priority. The created order has everything to do with our faith, because it has everything to do with God. Empires do not like to acknowledge this.

However, the very thing that has helped to accelerate our consumption and depletion of natural resources, globalisation, may well turn out to have a part to play in its salvation too. Via the Internet we are able to hear about people on the other side of the world, engage in conversation and debate with them. Together we have to find ways to live and relate differently. We must act locally, lobby nationally and think globally. In doing this we must guard against simplistic solutions on the one hand and avoid becoming cynical and apathetic on the other. Every little helps, and every little helps me to start living a different way, freeing myself up from patterns of addictive behaviour of needing yet more.[22]

Moving towards the margins

Leaders of well-established institutions and organisations are usually quite limited in how effectively they can facilitate change, unless they employ the tactics of empire: domination, manipulation and coercion. This approach is, of course, a form of violence. Whenever a new Archbishop of Canterbury is appointed some of my non-Anglican colleagues look at me as if to say, "Well, will this be the one who eventually sorts out the Church of England?" Every Archbishop has been quite clear about how limited they are in what they can personally achieve.

In my own way, I was a leader of an institution in Macclesfield. I led a team of churches with its staff, congregations, volunteers and wide range of activities. When I was a vicar in Birmingham, I led a small church which ran a large community project. For twelve years, I was chair of the companies that made up its social businesses, responsible for oversight of its forty staff and all its activities. Because of this, I am all too aware of how difficult it is sometimes to change an organisation once it has been established for any length of time. The pressure on leaders tends to become increasingly concerned with the affairs of the institution rather than what it was originally established for. They become more protective of the centre and more remote from the margins, the places where there is creative energy and the most interaction with the ordinary issues of life. However, it is on the edge, the margin, that God's Spirit is usually experienced as being at work. The best a leader can usually do is to set the "atmosphere" of an organisation that enables others to bring the necessary change. This has to be an atmosphere which encourages people to trust each other, take risks and forgive mistakes. To do this, it is crucial the leader makes himself or herself vulnerable and also becomes more in touch with what happens on the edges of their organisation.

At the beginning of his ministry, Jesus set a different atmosphere to that of the religious leaders and modelled this vulnerable movement towards the margins. A man with the devastating skin disease, leprosy, came and threw himself at the feet of Jesus, begging to be healed (Mark 1:40–45). Jesus then did what polite, religious society said he should not do—he touched the man. Jesus went against all regulations, laws and conventions. By touching the man he became unclean himself and was, therefore, shamed in the eyes of all who saw the incident. Jesus put himself in the position of the man as a social outcast on the margins of society. All through the Gospels Jesus reinforced this pattern of ministry from the margins.

Big and strong churches often feel they have something to offer the poor and the powerless. They may well have, but without realising it they easily adopt a patronising, even imperial, attitude. They regard those who are weaker and poorer, together with their church communities, as projects to be attended to, managed and solved. What is first needed is not activity, but solidarity. Solidarity is a very good word to replace "fellowship", which has been devalued and domesticated in the Christian world, robbed of its strong meaning. Fellowship is more than loving support and care. It is about solidarity. To become "solid" with others is to become completely one with them. It is about compassion, which means literally to share in another's pain. People are not usually poor and powerless through choice, but through lack of opportunity or misfortune. The more powerful, who have benefitted from opportunity and good fortune, need to adopt a new approach to those who are less powerful. They also need to realise that the pattern of mission in the New Testament is not from a strong and privileged centre towards a poor and weak edge. No, the mission of the church worked the other way round. It was from the margins to the centre (from Joppa to Jerusalem, from Galilee to Judea, from Judea to Rome).

Peter had to learn this lesson when he encountered the Roman centurion, Cornelius (Acts 10). God told Cornelius, a Gentile, to send men to bring Peter to his house, but Peter was not ready for this.

As Cornelius' men were on the road to meet him, Peter was praying his midday prayers on the roof of the place he was staying. He fell into a trance and had a dream where we saw a large sheet come down from heaven. It held an assortment of snakes, birds and other animals. Then a voice said, "Rise and eat." Peter could not do it. As a Jew, he knew these creatures were ritually unclean and so it was forbidden for him to eat them—but the voice said, "What God has made clean, you must not call profane." Twice more Peter was instructed to eat this food, and twice more, Peter hesitated.

Then, suddenly, the sheet with the birds of the air and slithery land reptiles was rapidly pulled back into the heavens and there was a knock

on the door. Two men stood there and asked him to come to the house of
Cornelius and accept his hospitality. Peter no longer hesitated, but went
to the home of a Gentile. In the great mission of God, Peter had to learn
to break free from what his family and his synagogue had taught him.

Peter had to learn that the distinctions of "them and us", of "clean and
unclean", of "Jew and Gentile" did not exist in the kingdom of God. All
Jews had to face the crisis that God's love and grace extended to the whole
world and they had not got an exclusive right to it. Peter had to face the
fact that what he had been told as a child was no longer adequate. The
theme of this unlearning and relearning from the margins is an endless
process which we hear echoed in the words of Paul: "There is no longer
Jew or Greek, there is no longer slave or free, there is no longer male and
female; for all of you are one in Christ Jesus" (Gal. 3:28). There are no
longer categories of status or privilege, of entitlement or priority in God's
way of doing things. As Peter entered the Gentile home of Cornelius he
left behind the belief the Jews were the only ones who had God's special
favour. It was when Peter and his fellow believers embraced this risky
newness that the Spirit of God was released; not in the certainties of
inherited traditions or the established habits of community behaviour.

In Acts 15, some believers came down from Judea (the centre) to
Antioch (the margins) to instruct the church, saying, "Unless you are
circumcised according to the custom of Moses, you cannot be saved"
(15:1). They also had to unlearn what they thought they knew, though.
Uncircumcised Gentiles, along with tax collectors and sinners, were to
be embraced by the church. The gospel does not operate as empires do,
which is from the centre and the top to the edges and the bottom. These
are the routes of domination and exploitation. In the kingdom of God,
the gift is to be found where it is least expected.

Because of this, I try to encourage church members in more affluent
communities to either move to, or at least get involved somehow with, a
church that is, on the face of it, weaker, smaller and more vulnerable than
theirs. The main reason for doing this is it will change them personally.
Initially, they think they will go and help "them" out, but do not realise
the possibility that the people they call "them" might actually do even
more for those who "go to help". Meeting the relatively powerless helps
us realise that the distance between our own perceived security and

disaster is quite short. I meet people whose marriages have broken up, who have been made redundant or who have faced unexpected serious illness. They tell me they can see how people who seem to have it all can easily end up on the street.

In 1986, I went to Birmingham to be a youthful, bright and shining vicar, to show others how urban ministry is really done. While I worked hard at what I thought I had to bring, I had to learn that what I saw in richer churches would not work in Bordesley Green. The experience was not always easy and sometimes it was humiliating, but eventually it taught me things about myself, my faith and the Bible that I would not have learnt otherwise. Only then did I really find my way forward in helping to lead the church.

The liberation theologian, Jon Sobrino, emphasised this point when he said anti-imperial theory understands that liberation comes from the victims of the empire.[23] This is the power of the powerless. In the Bible, salvation comes from the weak, the outsider and the excluded. God chose Israel (a constant victim of empire), a suffering servant, barren women, old people and children. Paul recognised that patronage was used by oppressive regimes to help empires retain their position. Our translations of the Bible often use the word "servant" as the word he applied to himself (Rom. 1:1, Gal. 1:10, Titus 1:1). The Greek word *doulos* properly means someone who belongs to another—a bond-slave; somebody without any ownership rights of their own. This is a bit more severe than our Western idea of a servant. Paul, like Jesus before him, repeatedly put himself in the place of somebody on the margins.

As churches we must practise solidarity with those who have lost out and been left behind in the globalising economic order. Too much of the "aid industry", nationally or internationally, is patronising. It is about doing something for (or even to) poor people to relieve them of their distress, not doing something with them. Not many people want to become one with the powerless in their struggle. We may not be able to become one with those overseas very easily, but we can start to experience solidarity with those who live across our town or city. This should always be our starting point.

Worship and the church

We have grown up with the idea that Christian worship generally happens in church services and meetings, and idolatry is the worship of carved images and statues. The English word "worship" is derived from Old English "worthscipe", meaning worthiness or worth-ship. Simply put, worship is to give worth to something. It can also be understood as anything we pledge our loyalty or allegiance to. In this book, I have observed that empires demand our loyalty and allegiance and, as such, our worship. They demand we take their hype, their products and their promises of security seriously. They enrol us in their mission of promoting their self-perceived goodness, as we swear loyalty to their brands. They co-opt us to their cause as we shell out good money to wear clothes emblazoned with their logos and symbols for others to see and admire. Unwittingly we get wrapped up in imperial worship, although we would not recognise it as such.

To find out what really is the object of our worship we must ask ourselves what we have pledged our loyalty and allegiance to. Using the language of spirituality, what are we "attached" to? In his letter to the Colossians, Paul was clear that greed is idolatry (Col. 3:5) and the Ten Commandments state idolatry is not God's way. Idolatry is as much alive today as in Biblical times. The danger is that we live lives enthralled by the ways of empire that surround us and then turn up to church on Sunday to worship God—but church services and religious buildings are not where worship begins. Worship starts at the place where our allegiance and loyalty lie. What we must ask is, to whom and to what do we give worth to each day? Services and rituals can only be an outward expression of worship that is already happening in our day-to-day living. Too often we have placed these things the other way round, assuming that if we get our worship services, meetings and rituals right, then our lives will fall into the right shape. Worship does not start in the sanctuary, but in the world.

Whatever our church denomination or tradition, we have a history that has been rooted in the Constantine establishment of Christianity with all of its imperial overtones. This institution, built on stability, authority, patronage and financial independence is now falling apart around us. We may feel we are becoming free of this heritage, but the spirit of empire continues to live on in the church, as it does in the culture we live in.

Just recently I had a prayer diary come through the post. One minister's request said, "We'd love prayer for our Sunday school, we'd really love it to grow!" Is this because they really love children or is it because they want a bigger Sunday school, I ask myself.

There is still a strong bias in us towards the big and growing. We still are not free from the expectations of empire. The church is called to model God's other way for all to see. It is not called to be a light to the nations by getting people to join it and sign up to its programmes and belief statements. It is called to be a prophetic witness to how things are in the kingdom of God and announce how things will ultimately be in a new heaven and earth. This is what the church has to proclaim. If we invite anybody to anything, it is to join this mission. Luke Timothy Johnson, a New Testament scholar and historian of early Christianity, challenges the church with these questions:

> Does the church have a prophetic vision with respect to power and possessions that challenge a world in which both economic and politics are so disordered? Or is the church too often co-opted by the world's vision rather than the prophet's in these areas?[24]

While the church is tied up with anxiety about its own survival it will not be able to play this prophetic role. The Biblical story tells us that newness is usually discovered in the wilderness of life, on the edge and in exile. God's people have rarely been volunteers for this agenda, although there have been many remarkable individuals who have embraced this. What has happened time and time again, when God's people have resisted exile and wilderness, is that exile and wilderness has come to them anyway. Then, and only then, has a new imagination emerged which has exhibited life, variety and freedom. Until then, imagination has been a scarce resource.

During the Chinese Cultural Revolution, the communist regime clamped down on the churches. From the outside it looked like they were doomed: they were no longer allowed to have paid pastors, buildings to worship in or hold meetings of more than fifteen people. Yet the church did not die. It thrived and found new life while in its own exile under the new empire of the Chinese communist state.

This should encourage us in two ways. It should persuade us to stop focussing on the success of our churches as our main purpose. It should also help us to believe that God is ultimately in control of the church. As Jesus said to his disciples when choosing Peter: "I will build my church."

In summary

It is too easy to read the Bible in a way that confirms our assumptions rather than challenges them. The passages that give us comfort are important, but we cannot ignore the fact that the Bible asks us to change our thinking and our preferred assumptions (i.e. repent). In this book, I have explained how the Bible does this by calling us to God's way of living, away from the empires of the world. As such, the Bible is an anti-imperial book.

We have all conspired and colluded with the empires and always will do, but hopefully less so as time goes by. Like Abraham, the Children of Israel, the disciples and the churches in the book of Revelation, we are called out of the way of life which enslaves us and into freedom. We are called to reclaim our God-given humanity and live as citizens of the alternative empire, becoming a prophetic people who refuse imperial powers' desire to imprison us. We are called to be a people of hope and resistance.

To do this, we must return to our roots and to simplicity. The Ten Commandments are our charter for anti-imperial living. Let us not allow people to use them as a measure of personal righteousness or to condemn others. It is on the principles of Sinai that the kingdom of God was built, and the kingdom of God was Jesus' main concern. This, then, should be our main concern too.

Questions for discussion

1. In what ways can contemplative prayer be subversive? In what ways can retreating into silence cause us to collude with the empires of the world?
2. Have we relied too much on attempting to control life? Has this affected our spirituality? Has this affected the way we do church?
3. When people say Christianity is a patriarchal religion, how do you respond? In what ways is it still patriarchal? How can we reduce abuse, oppression and injustice between men and women?
4. Which of the organisational models struck you as a fresh and life-giving approach? How can you promote justice in how you use your money? How can you live with less so the demand on the environment is less?
5. How can you spend more time with people on the margins in such a way you are not the more powerful person in the partnership? On a scale of 1 to 10, how anxious are church people about its survival? What has God called you: (a) out of, and (b) into for the next phase of your life?

Prayer

As the God who acts,
　　do something in our world,
　　our church and our lives, we pray.
Do something
that comes from beyond
　　our limited horizons,
　　and takes us beyond
　　our expectations.
Lift us
from our anxious and small worlds

to see the wonder and beauty
present
here today
in the people we meet
and all we see.
Amen.

Notes

1. Kenneth Leech, *Contemplation and Resistance*, in Robert Llewellyn (Ed.), *Circles of Silence: Explorations in Prayer with Julian Meetings* (Darton, Longman and Todd, 1994).

2. Reprinted with permission of the publisher. From *Finding our Way: Leadership for an Uncertain Time*, copyright© 2005 by Margaret J Wheatley, Berrett-Koehler Publishers, Inc., San Francisco, CA. p. 25. All rights reserved. <http://www.bkconnection.com>

3. For more detailed information see: <http://www.fawcettsociety.org.uk> and <http://www.womensaid.org.uk>.

4. Cath Elliott, "I'm not Praying", *The Guardian*, 19 August 2008. Copyright held by Guardian News and Media Limited.

5. Companies Act 2006 sections 171 to 177.

6. Henry Wallich, "Zero Growth", *Newsweek* Vol. 79, 24 January 1972, p. 62.

7. In 2013 and 2014 serious problems emerged in the Group. Its bank was found to have inadequate levels of capital, and subsequently other major issues arose about strategic decisions it had made and how the organisation was governed. Those governance issues are being resolved, but none of this detracts from the basic merit and strength of the mutual business model which continues to provide an alternative way of doing business to investor ownership, and is being used creatively in many new situations in the UK and around the world.

8. <http://www.mozilla.org>.

9. Examples include: The Linux Foundation, The Wikimedia Foundation (operating Wikipedia) and The Document Foundation (operating Libre Office).

10. <http://www.fairtrade.org.uk>.

11. <http://shopintideswell.co.uk>.

12. Carl Honore, *In Praise of Slow: How a Worldwide Movement is Challenging the Cult of Speed* (Orion, 2005).

13. I wonder if that is what Jesus is getting at in Matthew 25:29. If it is, then it requires a very different reading of the so-called parable of the talents which we normally interpret in support of our acquisitive culture.

14. Tom Hodgkinson, *How to be Idle* (Penguin, 2005), p. 248.

15. *The Economics of Failure: The real cost of 'free' trade for poor countries.* A Christian Aid briefing paper. June 2005.

16. *The Damage Done: Aid, Death and Dogma.* A Christian Aid briefing paper. May 2005.

17. This quote first appeared in Cafod and Christian Aid publication *A Human Development Approach to Globalisation* by Duncan Green and Claire Melamed in 2000, and is reproduced with its permission.

18. <http://www.amazon.com/review/R11Z8L8HTBGNDE>.

19. Lester R. Brown, *World on the Edge: How to Prevent Environmental and Economic Collapse* (Earthscan, 2011).

20. The Five Marks of Mission endorsed by Churches Together in England in 1996:
    - To proclaim the good news of the kingdom.
    - To teach, baptise and nurture new believers.
    - To respond to human need by loving service.
    - To seek to transform unjust structures of society.
    - To safeguard the integrity of creation, and sustain and renew the life of the earth.

21. "The Fifty Things That Will Save the Planet", *Your Environment Extra*, Issue 17, November 2007—January 2008. p. 17. Published by the Environment Agency. This can be viewed at <http://image.guardian.co.uk/sys-files/Environment/documents/2007/10/31/50top.pdf>.

22. Christian agencies such as A Rocha UK are a valuable resource to help us do this. See: <http://www.arocha.org>.

23. <http://portland.indymedia.org/en/2006/04/338511.shtml>.

24. Luke Timothy Johnson, *Prophetic Jesus, Prophetic Church: The Challenge of Luke-Acts to Contemporary Christians* (Eedrmans, 2011), p. 95.

The Last Word

A few months after taking up the post of team rector in Macclesfield, I was approached by a man at a concert, held in one of our churches, who asked, "Do you know who I am?" I immediately recognised him from forty years earlier; I even remembered his name. He was one of my secondary school teachers. I got the impression he was somewhat surprised to see me in a responsible position in the church, just as I was surprised to be bumping into one of my old adversaries.

I confessed to him that the school had not done me much good. He immediately responded by saying he had not fared well from the experience either. In fact, he had taken early retirement to escape. This led me to reflect on what I might say to any of the boys I was at school with if I ever met them unexpectedly.

Throughout my ministry I have met men who could have easily been my classmates all those years ago—women too if it had been a mixed school. Many of these men and women have muddled through life the best they could without meeting enough people to help and encourage them, nor having many "lucky breaks". I have been very fortunate, over the years, as there have been many people who have supported, accepted and loved me. Some were of valuable practical help to me as they had skills or contacts to help me. My parents taught me the faith and my family has always affirmed me and believed in what I have done. The world has treated me more than fairly; I can in no way claim to be a victim of injustice.

When I meet people who I could well have been at school with over forty years ago and who have not fared well, I want to affirm them and let them know something of the good news of the kingdom I have explored in this book. I want to deconstruct their preconceived ideas about God,

Jesus and the Biblical story. I want to tell them there really is good news for those who do not feel they have progressed through life very well.

I also realise what I have written can be disturbing to those who have done well and prospered in life. I find many of these ideas uncomfortable myself. But the truth is everyone needs liberating; no one is properly free until all are free. My healing and wholeness, freedom and fulfilment are bound together with my fellow human beings' well-being, whoever they are and wherever they may be.

For me, Jesus and the story of the Bible show us a God who brings to both rich and poor people freedom from all forms of slavery, hope in confusing and threatening times, and a sense of what it means to live a life from a contented inner spirit. This, I contend, is God's other way.

Bibliography

Alexander, Loveday, *Images of Empire* (Sheffield Academic Press, 1991).

Bauckham, Richard, *The Bible in Politics: How to Read the Bible Politically* (SPCK, 1989).

Bessey, Sarah, *Jesus Feminist: God's Radical Notion that Women are People, too* (Darton, Longman and Todd, 2013).

Brueggemann, Walter, *Hopeful Imagination: Prophetic Voices in Exile* (Fortress Press, 1986).

Brueggemann, Walter, *Finally Comes the Prophet: Daring Speech for Proclamation* (Fortress Press, 1989).

Brueggemann, Walter, *Out of Babylon* (Abingdon, 2010).

Crossan, John Dominic, *God and Empire: Jesus Against Rome, Then and Now* (Harper, 2007).

de Mello, Anthony, *The Way to Love* (Image, 1995).

de Waal, Esther, *A Seven Day Journey with Thomas Merton* (Eagle, 1992).

Hampson, Daphne (Ed.), *Swallowing a Fishbone: Feminist Theologians Debate Christianity* (SPCK, 1996).

Herschel, Abraham Joshua, *The Sabbath* (Farrar Straus Giroux, 2005).

Hodgkinson, Tom, *How to be Idle* (Penguin, 2005).

Honore, Carl, *In Praise of Slow: How a Worldwide Movement is Challenging the Cult of Speed* (Orion, 2005).

Horsley, Richard A. (Ed.), *Paul and Empire: Religion and Power in Roman Imperial Society* (Trinity Press, 1997).

Horsley, Richard A., *In the Shadow of Empire: Reclaiming the Bible as a History of Faithful Resistance* (Westminster John Knox, 2008).

Howard-Brook, Wes, *Come Out My People! God's Call Out of Empire in the Bible and Beyond* (Orbis, 2010).

Jamison, Christopher, *Finding Sanctuary: Monastic Steps for Everyday Life* (Weidenfeld & Nicolson, 2006).

Jamison, Christopher, *Finding Happiness* (Orion, 2008).

Johnson, Luke Timothy, *Prophetic Jesus, Prophetic Church: The Challenge of Luke-Acts to Contemporary Christians* (Eerdmans, 2011).

Lane, Belden, *The Solace of Fierce Landscapes: Exploring Desert and Mountain Spirituality* (Oxford University Press, 1998).

Llewelyn, Robert (Ed.), *Circles of Silence: Explorations in Prayer with Julian Meetings* (Darton, Longman and Todd, 1994).

McKnight, Scot and Modica, Joseph B. (Eds.), *Jesus is Lord, Caesar is Not: Evaluating Empire in New Testament Studies* (IVP Academic, 2013).

Merton, Thomas, *New Seeds of Contemplation* (New Directions, 1972).

Myers, Ched, *Binding the Strong Man: A Political Reading of Mark's Story of Jesus* (Orbis, 1988).

Myers, Ched; Dennis, Marie; Nangle, Joseph; Moe-Lobeda, Cynthia and Taylor, Stuart, *Say to this Mountain: Marks Story of Discipleship* (Orbis, 1996).

Palmer, Parker J., *Let Your Life Speak: Listening for the Voice of Vocation* (Jossey-Bass, 2000).

Redfern, Catherine and Aune, Kirstin, *Reclaiming the F Word: Feminism Today* (Zed Books, 2013).

Rohr, Richard, *Everything Belongs: The Gift of Contemplative Prayer* (Crossroad, 2003).

Rohr, Richard, *True Self False Self* (Compact Disc Edition) (St Anthony Messenger Press, 2003).

Rohr, Richard, *Falling Upwards: A Spirituality for the Two Halves of Life* (Jossey-Bass, 2011).

Rolheiser, Ronald, *The Shattered Lantern: Rediscovering the Felt Presence of God* (Hodder and Stoughton, 1994).

Sacks, Jonathan, *The Dignity of Difference: How to Avoid the Clash of Civilizations* (Continuum, 2002).

Shannon, William H. (Ed.), *The Inner Experience: Notes on Contemplation* (SPCK, 2003).

Tolle, Eckhart, *The Power of Now: A Guide to Spiritual Enlightenment* (Hodder and Stoughton, 1999).

Vincent, John (Ed.), *Acts in Practice* (Deo Publishing, 2012).

Wheatley, Margaret J., *Finding our Way: Leadership for an Uncertain Time* (Berrett-Koehler, 2005).

Whitworth, Patrick, *Prepare for Exile: A New Spirituality and Mission for the Church* (SPCK, 2008).

Wink, Walter, *Engaging the Powers: Discernment and Resistance in a World of Domination* (Fortress Press, 1992).

Wright, N. T., *The Challenge of Jesus* (SPCK, 2000).

Wright, Tom, *How God became King: Getting to the Heart of the Gospels* (SPCK, 2012).

Yancey, Philip, *The Bible Jesus Read* (Zondervan, 1999).

Yoder, John Howard, *The Politics of Jesus* (Paternoster Press, 1994).